# THE COMPLETE BOOK OF
# CREATIVE CRAFTS

THE COMPLETE BOOK OF

# CREATIVE
# CRAFTS

PARRAGON

## HOW TO USE THE MEASUREMENTS

*All craftspeople have their own way of working and feel most comfortable calculating in their preferred measurements. So, where applicable, the option of metric, imperial and cup measures are given. The golden rule is to choose only one set of measurements and to stick with it throughout each project to ensure accurate results.*

## PUBLISHER'S NOTE

*Crafts and hobbies are great fun to learn and can fill many hours of rewarding leisure time, but some general points should be remembered for safety and care of the environment.*

- *Always choose non-toxic materials wherever possible, for example paints, glue and varnishes. Where these are not suitable, use materials in a well-ventilated area and always follow the manufacturer's instructions.*

- *Craft knives, needles, scissors, sewing machines and all sharp implements should be used with care. Always use a cutting board or mat to avoid damage to household surfaces (it is also safer to cut onto a firm, hard surface).*

- *Protect surfaces from paint, glue and varnish splashes by laying down old newspapers, plastic sheeting or an old sheet.*

## SOME USEFUL TERMS

| US | UK |
|---|---|
| *Clear rubbing alcohol* | *White spirit* |
| *Flat latex* | *Matt emulsion paint* |
| *Grease pencil* | *Chinagraph pencil* |
| *Heavy-weight iron-on fabric* | *Heavy pelmet vilene* |
| *Posterboard* | *Card* |
| *Styrofoam* | *Polystyrene* |
| *Upholstery fabric* | *Furnishing fabric* |
| *White glue* | *PVA glue* |
| *Zipper* | *Zip* |

This edition published in 1997 by
Parragon
Units 13-17
Avonbridge Trading Estate
Atlantic Road
Avonmouth
Bristol BS11 9QD

© Anness Publishing Limited 1992, 1995

Produced by
Anness Publishing Limited
Hermes House, 88-89 Blackfriars Road,
London SE1 8HA

ISBN  0-75252-153-5 (hardback)
ISBN  0-75252-164-0 (paperback)

Printed and bound in Italy

# CONTENTS

# FABRIC CRAFTS

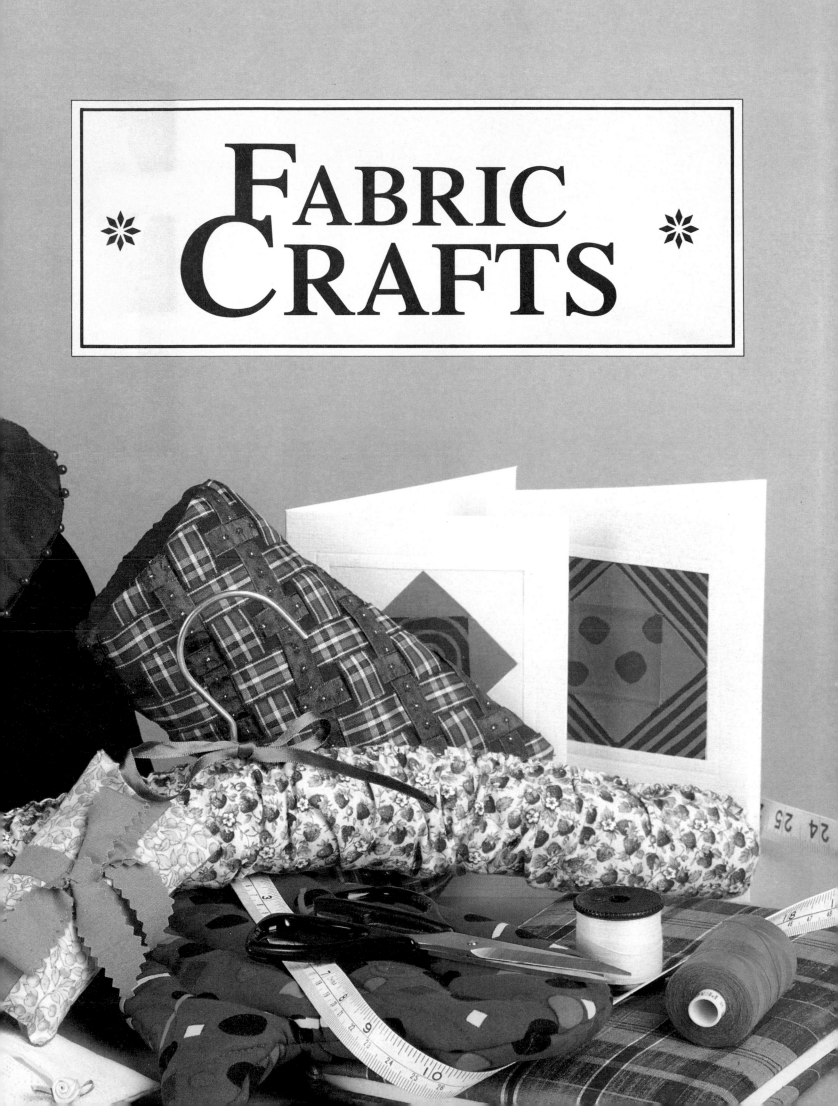

# TINY TRINKET BOX

A little triangular tartan box, lined with silk, would make a delightful gift either on its own or containing a tiny surprise.

## YOU WILL NEED
*Tracing paper*
*Pencil*
*Template plastic*
*50 cm (½ yd) fusible woven heavy-weight iron-on interlining*
*Scissors*
*25 cm (10 in) square of tartan fabric*
*25 cm (10 in) square of silk fabric for lining*
*50 cm (½ yd) square of brushed cotton for interlining*
*Steam iron*
*Needle and thread*

**1** Size up and trace the triangular and oblong shapes onto template plastic. Using a sharp pencil, draw four triangles and six oblongs on the iron-on interlining. Cut them out, then slightly trim two of the triangles and three of the oblongs for the lining.

**2** Cut out two triangles and three oblongs from the tartan and lining silk leaving a 6 mm (¼ in) seam allowance all round. Cut double the amount from the brushed cotton but without seam allowances.

**3** Place the tartan pieces wrong side up on an ironing board. Cover them with the brushed cotton pieces, then the iron-on interlining, sticky side up. Press the fabric seam allowance up onto the sticky side with the tip of the iron. Leave to cool. Repeat with the silk lining pieces.

**4** Press the tartan fronts and silk linings together, wrong sides facing, until they fuse. Leave to cool. Whip stitch the pieces in place.

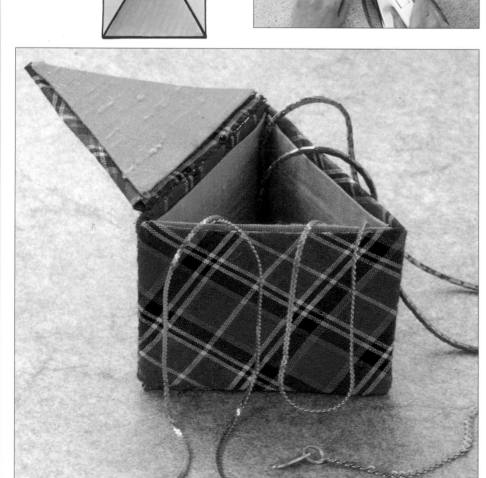

**5** Whip stitch the three sides of the box to the base, right sides together. Pull up the sides of the box and slip stitch together. Slip stitch along the hinge of the lid.

# NAPKIN RINGS AND NAPKINS

Matching napkin rings and napkins give a table a festive look for a special lunch or dinner party. These are quick to make using tartan ribbons and pelmet interlining.

## YOU WILL NEED

25 cm (¼ yd) fusible woven heavy-weight iron-on interlining
Scissors
2 m × 12 mm (2 yd × ½ in) tartan ribbon
Iron
Stapler
Needle and thread
1 m × 115 cm (1 yd × 45 in) red fabric

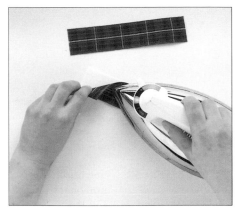

**1** For each napkin ring, cut out a piece of iron-on interlining 15 cm × 4 cm (6 in × 1½ in) and a matching length of tartan ribbon. Iron the ribbon onto the sticky side of the pelmet interlining. Leave to cool.

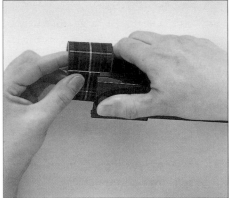

**2** Bend into a circle and secure with two staples.

**3** Make a looped decoration with the tartan ribbon and sew in place over the join. Cut the ends of the ribbon diagonally.

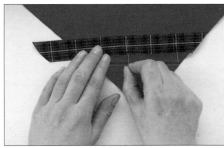

**4** Cut out four napkins 45 cm (18 in) square in the red fabric. Sew a strip of tartan ribbon diagonally across one corner of each napkin.

**5** Trim all the corners diagonally to reduce bulk. Turn in a small hem and sew. Press well.

# EVENING TOTE-BAG

Jewel-coloured velvet is the ideal fabric for this capacious evening tote-bag. Twisted gold knitting yarn forms the cord.

## YOU WILL NEED
Tracing paper
Pencil
Stencil card
Craft knife
Double-sided tape
Scissors
50 cm × 152 cm (½ yd × 60 in) velvet
Paper
Masking tape
Gold spray paint
Gold knitting yarn for the cord
50 cm × 115 cm (½ yd × 45 in) gold lining
Pins
Needle and thread
Safety pin or bodkin
Gilt bead

**1** Scale up and trace the fleur-de-lys template. Scribble on the back of the paper with a soft pencil to make a carbon. Turn over and draw over the lines of the motif onto stencil card. Cut out the motif with a craft knife. Stick small pieces of double-sided sticky tape on the back to hold the stencil onto the fabric.

**2** Cut out two pieces of velvet 55 cm × 38 cm (21½ in × 15 in). Centre the stencil motif on the fabric and press gently so that the sticky tape holds. Place paper over the remaining fabric to prevent the paint from spreading and hold in place with masking tape. Shake the can of spray paint according to the manufacturer's instructions. Spray and leave to dry thoroughly before removing the stencil.

**3** Meanwhile, make a twisted cord. Measure out 8 strands of yarn, each 4.5 m (15 ft) long, which will give you a finished length of about 2 m (6 ft 6 in). Hook the strands of yarn at one end over a window catch or door handle, and tie a knot in the other end. Slip a pencil through the end and twist tightly until the yarn forms a cord. Tie a knot at the other end, then tie another two knots about 10 cm (4 in) from one end. Cut between these two knots, and use this 10 cm (4 in) length to make a loop.

**4** Cut out two pieces of lining 55 cm × 38 cm (21½ in × 15 in). Pin the linings to the tops of each of the velvet pieces.

**5** Pin the cord loop to the right side of the velvet near the bottom.

**6** Place the two pieces right sides together and pin, then tack, around three sides, leaving a gap open at the bottom of the linings. This will enable you to turn it through. Turn through to the right side and make a double seam along the bottom of the lining to close.

**7** Tuck the lining into the bag and tack along the top edge, and again 5 cm (2 in) further down. Machine two lines next to this tacking line, about 2.5 cm (1 in) apart to form a channel. Open a few stitches in one seam so that the cord can pass through the channel. Thread through, using a bodkin or a safety pin.

**8** Pass both ends of the cord through a gilt bead, then through the loop. Tie the ends together and cut to form a tassel.

# DUCK PINCUSHION

A firm and colourful duck to keep all your pins out of trouble, easily made from oddments of material and decorated in different ways. Silk or felt are particularly effective fabrics to work with.

## YOU WILL NEED
Metal rule
Plain paper
Pencil
Scissors
Pins
Piece of left-over fabric, about 38 cm × 28 cm (15 in × 11 in)
Needle and thread
Polyester stuffing (batting)
2 small glass beads
30 cm × 12 mm (12 in × ½ in) ribbon

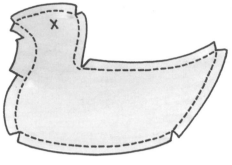

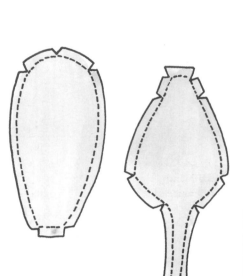

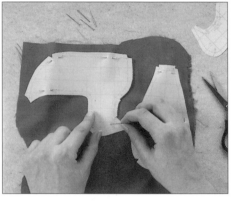

**1** Scale up the template, transfer onto paper and cut out. Pin the patterns onto the fabric and cut out, leaving 6 mm (¼ in) all round each piece for the seam allowances.

**2** Pin the four pieces together and stitch along the joins, leaving the front of neck open where marked. Turn the duck inside out and push the stuffing (batting) through the neck hole until the duck is firm. Sew on the glass beads for the eyes. Sew up the neck hole and cover the join with a piece of ribbon. Pleat remaining ribbon and add to the tail.

# BOLSTER CUSHION

Brighten up your living room with an elegant bolster cushion, using a patterned furnishing fabric that reflects your colour scheme.

## YOU WILL NEED

*Tape measure*
*Bolster cushion, about 45 cm (18 in) long*
*Furnishing fabric to fit cushion*
*Scissors*
*Iron*
*Zip about 41 cm (16 in)*
*Pins*
*Needle and thread*
*Thin card*
*Wadding (batting) for end circles*
*30 cm (12 in) square of silk for end circles*
*Fray check liquid*

**1** Measure the length and circumference of the cushion.

**2** Cut out the fabric to these measurements adding seam allowances. Press in these allowances, one 12 mm (½ in) and one 15 mm (⅝ in), on two opposite long sides. Mark the centre of sides and of the zip. Pin, tack (baste) and sew in place using a zipper foot if sewing by machine. The side with the smaller seam allowance should be sewn with the zip closed and the other side with the zip open.

**3** Turn the cover through and insert the cushion, centrally. Pleat into folds and pin the two ends. Take out the cushion and sew the pleats in place.

**4** Cut out two circles of card about 5 cm (2 in) in diameter and two circles of wadding (batting) the same size. Cut out two of silk 10 cm (4 in) in diameter. Apply fray check and run a tacking (basting) stitch just inside one silk circle.

**5** Place over a card circle and wadding (batting), pulling up the thread to tighten and finishing with a knot. Repeat with the other silk circle. Insert the bolster cushion into the cover. Pin a covered circle in the centre of each end and stitch in place.

# VELVET PURSE

Unusual evening bags, just large enough for lipstick, comb and purse are hard to find. Here velvet and silk are combined to give the finishing touch to a party outfit.

## YOU WILL NEED
*Tracing paper*
*Pencil*
*Scissors*
*Pins*
*30 cm × 115 cm (⅓ yd × 45 in) velvet*
*30 cm × 115 cm (⅓ yd × 45 in) silk*
*Needle and thread*
*Lurex knitting yarn*
*Safety pin or bodkin*
*Pearl beads*

**1** Using the template for guidance, transfer the pattern onto tracing paper to measure 43 cm (17 in) from base to tip by 25 cm (10 in) wide. Place on the velvet and cut out two pieces, making sure that the pile of the fabric lies the same way on both pieces. Cut out two lining pieces from the silk. Pin and tack (baste) the 'points' right sides together. Machine sew and trim the tip. Turn through and tack (baste) along the edges.

**2** Keeping the 'points' out of the way, join the fronts of the velvet and the silk lining together. Machine sew, leaving the base of the lining open for turning.

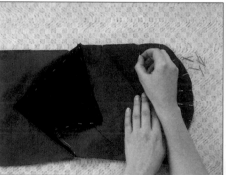

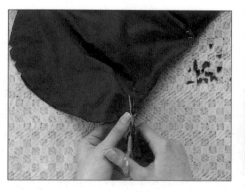

**3** Before turning, snip 'V' shapes out of the seam allowance around the curves, taking care not to snip the stitching.

**4** Turn the bag through, by putting your hand inside, grasping the base and pulling. Close the lining with a seam and tuck it into the bag.

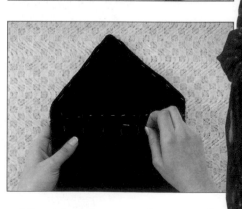

**5** Smooth the bag so that the two fabrics lie flat, then pin and run two lines of tacking (basting) as shown on the pattern. Sew along these lines which will form the channel for the cord.

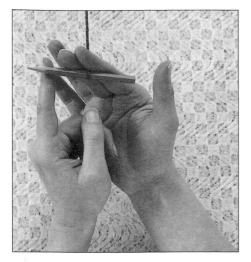

**6** Make the twisted cord by knotting eight strands of lurex knitting yarn about 90 cm (36 in) long to a hook or drawer knob. Stretch the yarn out and knot the ends together, then trim. Place a pencil in the loop and twist in one direction until the yarn is sufficiently tightly twisted to curl into a firm cord. Mark the centre, then knot the other ends. These cords are easier to make with two people twisting in opposite directions!

**7** Undo a couple of stitches along one side of the seam and using a safety pin or bodkin thread the cord through.

**8** Knot both ends together, then cut to make a tassel. If you would prefer a shoulder strap, make the cord longer. Decorate with pearls sewn along the edges of the 'points'. Remove the tacking (basting) threads.

# DIARY COVER

Diaries often have dull covers, so here is a way to personalize them using brightly coloured checked silk.

YOU WILL NEED
*Diary*
*Plain paper*
*Pencil*
*Ruler*
*Scissors*
*30 cm × 115 cm (⅓ yd × 45 in) silk*
*Fray check liquid*
*Double-sided tape*
*2 pieces of wadding (batting) to fit*
*Pins*
*Needle and thread*

**1** Measure the diary by placing it on a large piece of paper and drawing around the open front, spine and back. Add a fold allowance of 4 cm (1½ in). Cut out the paper and place it on the silk. Using a soft pencil, draw the shape.

**2** Cut out the silk and use a fray check liquid along the edges to prevent the silk fraying.

**3** Put a couple of pieces of double-sided tape on each side of the diary cover.

**4** Remove the backing paper from the tape and wrap the wadding (batting) around the diary, pressing onto the tape.

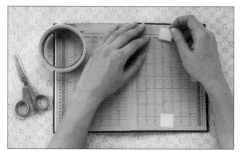

**5** Place some pieces of double-sided tape around the edges of the inside cover, peel off the backing paper and wrap the silk around, making sure you have an equal amount of fabric on each side to fold in.

**6** Make a diagonal cut on each side of the spine and fold the corners diagonally by tucking the spare fabric under.

**7** Fold the corners of the silk in and fold the edges over diagonally. Pin in place. Hold in place with a slip stitch, trimming the spine a little further if necessary.

# FABRIC LAMPSHADE

Trim a lampshade frame to match your living room in contrasting or co-ordinating fabric. Short lengths of left-over material are very useful for this type of project, and you can choose the size of wire frame according to the amount of fabric available. Be sure not to use a fabric that has a very low resistance to heat, such as some man-made fibres.

## YOU WILL NEED
*Wire lampshade frame*
*Tape measure*
*Length of fabric to cover frame with a*
  *seam allowance of 5 cm (2 in)*
*Same amount of pale lining fabric*
*Scissors*
*Pins*
*Needle and thread*
*Safety pin*
*Length of elastic equal to length of*
  *fabric*
*Braid to trim*

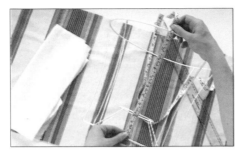

**1** To determine the amount of fabric needed, measure the height of the wire frame and its circum-ference. Add 5 cm (2 in) for the seam allowance. Cut the lining fabric to the same dimensions.

**2** Turn over the top and bottom seam allowances on both pieces and pin. Sew the edges of the two pieces of fabric together on the top only; sew two lines of stitches, leaving a channel for the elastic.

**3** Attach a safety pin to one end of the elastic and thread it through the channel, keeping hold of the other end. Holding the two ends together, place the main fabric over the shade, pull the elastic tight so that the shade sits well on the frame and sew the ends of the elastic together. Stitch up the seam in the fabric.

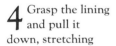

**4** Grasp the lining and pull it down, stretching the main fabric taut over the frame.

**5** Tuck the lining down inside the shade, and pin and sew in place at the top. Trim the edges with braid.

# DRAUGHT EXCLUDER

Make your home cosy and keep draughts at bay in a colourful way. Cushions in matching fabric would give a co-ordinated look.

## YOU WILL NEED
*Ruler*
*25 cm × 122 cm (¼ yd × 48 in)*
*  furnishing fabric*
*Scissors*
*Pins*
*Needle and thread*
*Wadding (batting) or stuffing*
*1.6 m (1¾ yd) wide ribbon*

**1** Measure the width of the door; upstairs doors are usually narrower than those downstairs. Allow an extra 18 cm (7 in) width for seam allowances and cut out the fabric to the required size. Turn in and pin 9 cm (3½ in) at each end and machine sew two rows of a long (gathering) stitch, stopping just short of the seam allowance. Pull the threads through to the right side of the fabric.

**2** Fold in half lengthways, right sides together. Pin and machine along the edge, taking care not to stitch over the long threads.

**3** Turn through to the right side and pull up the gathering threads at one end. Knot to fasten off.

**4** Stuff from the open end until the 'sausage' feels firm. Pull up the gathering threads from the open end. Tie securely and fasten off.

**5** Cut the ribbon in half and cut a 'V' shape in the ends. Tie an extravagant bow at each end of the 'sausage'.

# LACE HANDKERCHIEF

It is very simple to add delicate detail to a plain handkerchief with a trimming of lace. Scraps of unusual or antique lace are worth collecting and saving for such a project.

## YOU WILL NEED
*21 cm (8½ in) square of Swiss lawn
(fine cotton)*
*Steam iron*
*Tailor's chalk*
*Scissors*
*130 cm (51 in) fine cotton lace*
*Needle and thread*

**1** Fold the square of lawn into a triangle and press. Fold again to make a smaller triangle.

Unfold once. Chalk the position of the lace inside one corner, chalking on both sides.

**2** Cut off the corner of lawn along the chalked lines.

**3** Pin a strip of lace along the raw edge allowing a 6 mm (¼ in) overlap on the lawn. Pin the lawn corner to the lace again allowing a 6 mm (¼ in)

overlap. Secure with oversewing. Turn in the lawn overlap making a fine rolled hem along both sides, catching the edge of the lace at the same time.

**4** Sew four pieces of lace, each 28 cm (11 in) long, along each side of the handkerchief, leaving a 6 mm (¼ in) overlap. At each corner leave enough lace to overlap into a square. Trim the lace along the diagonal at each corner leaving 3 mm (⅛ in) overlapping. Hem the lawn overlap into a fine rolled edge along all four sides of the handkerchief. Neatly sew up the diagonal lace corners and sew the lace onto the hemmed edges.

### Working by hand

Although some appliqué designs are worked with machine satin stitch, you can work the stitching by hand if you prefer. Follow the project instructions in the usual way, but substitute buttonhole stitch for machine satin stitch. Work the stitch in a suitable embroidery thread such as stranded cotton.

### Working machine appliqué

Always work a small practice piece before starting to machine stitch or machine appliqué in order to check that your thread, needle, stitch size and fabric are compatible. Fit a new needle before starting to sew as a blunt one will damage the fabric and result in uneven stitching.

To work satin stitch, set your machine to a zigzag stitch about 3 mm (⅛ in) wide and 6 mm (¼ in) long. Use a special appliqué foot if one is provided with your machine. Test the stitch on a spare piece of fabric, practising points and corners, and adjust your machine as necessary. A piece of typing paper placed beneath your fabric on top of the sewing machine plate will help when puckering is a problem – stitch the design then tear away the paper round the stitches.

Start stitching at the beginning of a straight edge and do not go too fast. When working intricate shapes, go carefully and turn the wheel by hand to make one stitch at a time. Pivot at the corner of shapes by leaving the needle in the fabric, raising the presser foot and turning the fabric before lowering the foot and continuing to stitch. Never turn the wheel of the machine backwards as this will damage the machine.

### Using fusible bonding paper

Cut out a piece of fusible, iron-on bonding paper slightly larger than the shape to be applied. Cover the wrong side of the shape with the paper, placing it adhesive side down. Press

in place, setting the iron to the correct temperature for the fabric. Allow to cool, then cut out the shape. Peel off the backing paper and place the shape with the adhesive side down onto the right side of the background fabric. Carefully press the shape in place using either a steam iron or a dry iron and a damp cloth. Make sure you allow the fabric to dry thoroughly before you begin to stitch.

### Blanket stitch

Use blanket stitch for appliqué when working with a fabric such as felt which does not fray. When applying other types of fabric by hand, choose buttonhole stitch instead.

Work blanket stitch from left to right, pulling the needle through the fabric over the top of the working thread. Space the stitches evenly along the row.

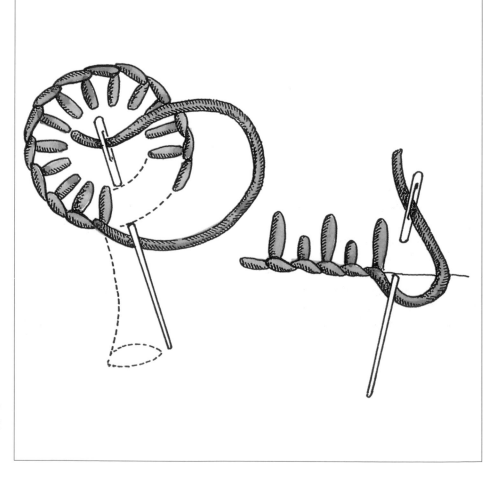

## Satin stitch

Use satin stitch to fill small shapes with stitching.

Take large stitches across the surface of the fabric, as shown, then return the thread underneath the fabric and bring the needle out close to the previous stitch. Work the stitches close together so the fabric is adequately covered.

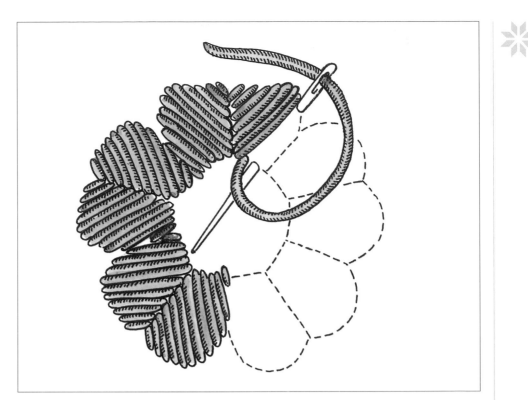

## Running stitch

This is the most basic embroidery stitch and you can achieve varying effects by altering the spacing between the stitches.

Work running stitch by passing the needle smoothly in and out of the fabric.

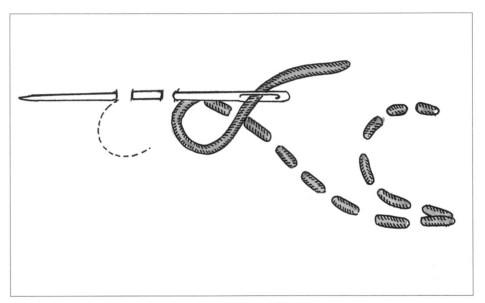

## Buttonhole stitch

Use buttonhole stitch as an edging stitch for appliqué.

Work buttonhole stitch from left to right in the same way as blanket stitch, pulling the needle through the fabric over the top of the working thread. Work the stitches close together so that no fabric is visible between them.

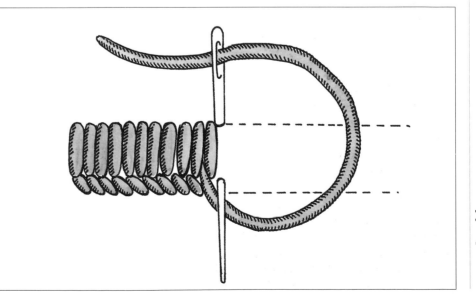

# STRAWBERRY BERET

Berets are available in a wide range of colours and are not expensive. Appliquéd felt strawberries make an original decoration for this classic yet elegant hat.

## YOU WILL NEED
*Red and green felt*
*Scissors*
*Needle and thread*
*Miniature beads*
*Beret*
*Rubber-based glue*

**1** Cut out some red strawberry shapes and green stems from the felt.

**2** Sew some beads onto each strawberry.

**3** Stick the motifs on the beret using rubber-based glue. Allow to dry.

# BERIBBONED SPECTACLE CASE

Make this pretty padded case to protect a pair of glasses. Choose brightly coloured fabric and ribbons so that the case will always be easy to find!

## YOU WILL NEED

*4 pieces of fabric, each measuring 14 cm × 21 cm (5½ in × 8½ in)*

*2 pieces of foam interlining, each measuring 14 cm × 21 cm (5½ in × 8½ in)*

*Pins*

*Needle and thread*

*Metal rule*

*Scissors*

*1.6 m (64 in) length of wide ribbon*

*1.6 m (64 in) length of narrow ribbon*

**1** Place a rectangle of fabric on top of each piece of foam interlining so that they fit flush. Pin and tack (baste) in place.

**2** Place the rectangles of fabric together. Pin and tack (baste). Sew around three sides with a 15 mm (⅝ in) seam allowance, leaving one short end open. Trim the seams. To make the ribbon front mark the front edge on the right side of one of the remaining rectangles of fabric 5 cm (2 in) from the top. Lay the first piece of ribbon from the corner to the mark. Secure with pins. Continue to lay the ribbon diagonally across the fabric, alternating the wide and narrow ribbons and leaving a gap of 5 mm (¼ in) between each ribbon. When you have reached the bottom of the material, do not forget to finish the top triangle. Tack (baste) into place.

**3** Next, start weaving the ribbon in the opposite direction, again alternating between the narrow and wide ribbons. Secure with pins. When complete, tack (baste) into place and trim the ends.

**4** Sew the ribbon side to the right side of the fabric rectangle. Sew around three sides, using a 20 mm (¾ in) allowance and leaving the bottom end open. Trim and turn through.

**5** Use a closed pair of scissors to push the lining gently and carefully into place. Turn the raw ends under by 3 cm (1¼ in). Pin and stitch in place.

# PATCH POCKET

This heart-shaped pocket in red felt looks very striking on a dark dress. Be sure to use a washable felt unless the dress has to be dry-cleaned.

### YOU WILL NEED
*Red felt*
*Scissors*
*Tracing paper*
*Pencil*
*Needle*
*Green and white embroidery thread*

**1** Cut out two heart shapes from the red felt and one in tracing paper. Draw a flower on the paper heart and trace the design onto one of the felt hearts.

**2** Stitch the stem using green embroidery thread.

**3** Stitch the flowers using white embroidery thread.

**4** Using blanket stitch and green embroidery thread, sew the two hearts together to form a pocket and then sew into place on the dress.

# APPLIQUÉD T-SHIRT

A plain white T-shirt can be quickly brightened up and made stylish enough for a gift, using appliquéd felt and jazzy beads. For a more ornate look, reduce the spacing between the beads or add longer stripes in the same pattern.

## YOU WILL NEED
*Tape measure*
*White T-shirt*
*Pins*
*Needle and tacking (basting) thread*
*Remnants of brightly coloured felt*
*Scissors*
*Embroidery thread*
*Beads and sequins*
*Steam iron*

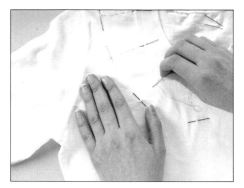

**1** Measure the neck opening of the T-shirt and mark the centre front with a pin. From this point, measure and pin every 5 cm (2 in) around the front of the neck opening. From each pin, measure down 5 cm (2 in) and mark with another pin. Tack (baste) between the pins with small stitches. Remove the pins.

**2** Cut out 14 felt circles, about 20 mm (¾ in) in diameter. Pin one at each end of the tacking (basting) stitches and another about 12 mm (½ in) along. Blanket stitch each circle of felt in position, using a contrasting colour of embroidery thread. Sew the beads and sequins between the circles. Remove the tacking (basting) and press.

# CHARACTER CUSHION

This cushion with a stylized appliquéd animal head is ideal for a child's room. Fine features are worked in a satin stitch. Remember to choose fabrics of similar weights and make sure they are all machine washable.

## YOU WILL NEED
*Ruler*
*Tracing paper*
*Pencil*
*Scissors*
*Pins*
*30 cm (12 in) square beige fabric for head*
*Remnants of green, pink, white and black fabric*
*50 cm × 1 m (½ yd × 39 in) blue fabric for features*
*Needle and thread*
*36 cm (14 in) cushion pad*

**1** Scale up the template to the required size. Trace over each separate section of the design, label for colour and cut out the shape. Pin each piece of tracing paper onto the correct colour fabric and cut out.

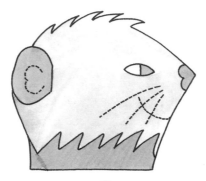

**2** Cut out a 36 cm (14 in) square of the blue fabric for the front of the cushion, including 3 cm (1¼ in) seam allowance. Pin the different coloured pieces onto this square, adjusting if necessary.

**3** Sew each piece into place using a running stitch. Go over the running stitches with a satin, close-set zigzag stitch. When all the material is sewn into place, sew on the other features such as whiskers and remove the pins.

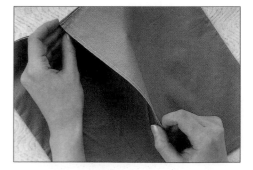

**4** To complete the cushion, cut the remaining blue fabric into two pieces, each measuring 36 cm × 24 cm (14 in × 9½ in) to allow for overlaps. Sew the pieces of fabric onto the back of the appliquéd panel so that the edges overlap forming an envelope. Insert the cushion pad.

# BROIDERY PERSE APRON

The appliqué roses on this apron will bring summer memories to the kitchen all the year round. The roses shown here were taken from a sample of furnishing fabric; they were applied using fusible bonding paper and satin stitched on the machine.

## YOU WILL NEED

1 m × 115 cm (1 yd × 45 in) striped fabric
Scissors
Fusible iron-on bonding paper
Piece of printed fabric with some large flowers
Steam iron
Tape measure
1.5 m (60 in) tape or ribbon for ties
Pins

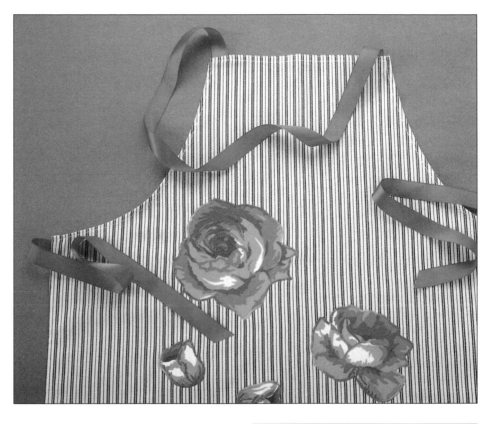

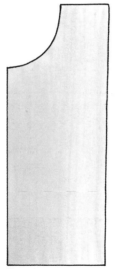

Fabric folded double

**2** Trim around the edge of the flowers.

**1** Scale up the template and transfer to striped fabric. Cut out. Cut out large enough pieces of fusible bonding paper to cover the chosen flowers and apply to the wrong side of the printed fabric using a steam iron. Measure the length of tape or ribbon required for the head loop and cut. Divide the remaining ribbon in half for the waist ties and cut the ends diagonally.

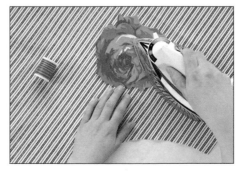

**3** Peel off the backing paper, then iron the flowers onto the front of the apron. Machine satin stitch around the flowers. It will help to keep the stitches flat if you place a piece of paper between the plate of the sewing machine and the back of the fabric. This may be torn away afterwards.

**4** Pin the waist ties and head loop in position, then turn in a small hem and machine stitch all the way round the apron. Reinforce the head loop with an extra row of machine stitches.

# APPLIQUÉD POT HOLDER

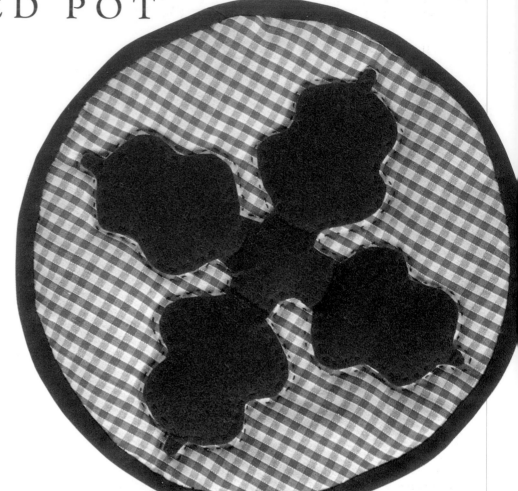

The technique used for making this decorative pot holder is known as Hawaiian appliqué. By using felt for the motif, there is no need to hem it which saves time. Remember to buy washable felt as pot holders need washing frequently!

## YOU WILL NEED
*Tracing paper*
*Pencil*
*Pins*
*20 cm (8 in) square of washable felt*
*Scissors*
*Plain paper*
*25 cm × 115 cm (¼ yd × 45 in) gingham*
*Square of double-thickness wadding (batting)*
*Needle and thread*
*Iron*
*Bias binding*

**1** Design a motif and trace it. Pin it onto the felt and cut it out. Cut out a circle in plain paper and place on the gingham. Using the paper template as a guide cut out two gingham circles.

**2** Centre the felt motif on one gingham circle and pin, then tack in place. Appliqué, with a small running stitch, just inside the motif. Press gently when finished.

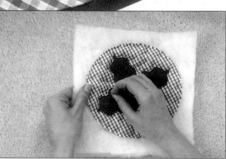

**3** Place the back, wadding (batting) and top together, then pin. Quilt with a small running stitch, just outside the motif.

**4** Pin firmly, then tack around the edge of the circle. Trim away the excess wadding (batting).

**5** Measure the circumference of the pot holder and cut a slightly longer strip of bias binding. Make a loop with more bias binding and pin to the pot holder.

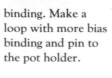

**6** Join the two ends of the bias binding strip with a diagonal seam, and fold the bias binding around the pot holder. Pin, tack and sew either by machine or by hand.

# TABLE RUNNER

This runner will decorate and protect the centre of any dining-room table while not in use. All the motifs are slightly different so you can cut out by eye and arrange the pieces as you go along. If you want to plan to size, cut out a piece of paper to the same dimensions as the table top and lay pieces of tracing paper cut to shape on top.

## YOU WILL NEED
*Felt in an assortment of colours*
*Scissors*
*Contrasting embroidery thread*
*Needle*
*Small pearl buttons*

**1** Cut out enough large and small felt hearts in contrasting colours to fill the outer diamonds of the pattern. Place a small heart in the centre of a large heart and join in the centre with a few stitches of embroidery thread.

**2** Sew around the edges of the small heart in blanket stitch.

**3** Cut a rectangle of felt to fit the size of the table. Cut out the diamonds that will go around the outer edge of the runner. Place the pair of hearts in the centre of the diamond and sew on using blanket stitch. Make up the floral motifs for the inner diamonds in the same way using coloured felt and blanket stitch.

**4** Position all the diamonds on the felt background. Attach the diamonds by the corners, stitching one small pearl button at the same time onto each corner. Add extra buttons for decoration on the floral motifs.

# HEART MOBILE

This pretty heart mobile glistens and sparkles as it moves, catching the light on the beads and jewels. Use contrasting colours of felt and vary the sizes of the hearts to create an eye-catching effect.

## YOU WILL NEED
*Plain paper*
*Pencil*
*Pinking shears*
*Pins*
*25 cm (10 in) squares of felt in bright colours*
*50 cm (½ yd) of 60 g (2 oz) wadding (batting), optional*
*Needle and embroidery thread*
*Scissors*
*Assortment of imitation jewels, beads and sequins*
*Coat hanger*

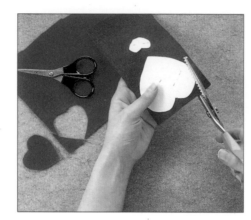

**1** Draw heart shapes of different sizes on paper and cut out the patterns using pinking shears. Pin the patterns onto the felt squares, and cut out a front and a back for each large heart shape. Cut out a medium-sized heart shape for each large heart, and a piece of wadding (batting), if stuffing the hearts.

**2** Decorate each tiny heart with imitation jewels, pressing the studs over each jewel to hold it in place. Sew on using brightly coloured thread and running stitch.

**3** Sew a tiny heart onto each medium-sized heart.

**4** Sew each medium-sized heart onto a large heart. Decorate both the front and the back of each motif.

**5** Sew each front and back together using a running stitch as close to the edge as possible, leaving a small gap to insert the wadding (batting) if using. Tie the hearts onto a coat hanger that can then be moved from place to place to catch the draught.

Appliqué

# VALENTINE BROOCH
# AND EARRINGS

Tell someone you love them by making these hand-stitched valentine earrings and brooch. You could use fabric for the appliqué, although felt is much easier to use as it does not fray.

### YOU WILL NEED
*Tracing paper*
*Black felt-tip pen*
*Scissors*
*Oddments of brightly coloured felt*
*Needle and thread*
*2 short headpins*
*Fabric glue*
*Sequins*
*2 kidney wires or ear-clips*
*Oddment of cotton fabric*
*Pins*
*Stuffing (batting)*
*3cm (1¼ in) straight brooch clip*

**1** For the earrings, scale up the hand and heart templates, transfer to the felt and cut out two hands and one heart. Using very small stitches, sew the heart in the centre of the hand.

**2** Sew one side of the hands together. Position a headpin in the middle so that the end protrudes. Glue in place. Sew the edges of the hand and figures together. Glue sequins onto the fingertips and one in the centre of the hand. Hang the earrings on a kidney wire or ear-clip. Repeat for the other earring, making sure that the hand and heart face in the opposite direction.

**3** For the brooch, cut out the small rectangular paper base template. Cut out one piece of fabric, and one of felt for the brooch back. Trace the geometric templates numbered 1–9 and cut out of fabric, leaving a small seam allowance around each shape. Pin them in place on the fabric front and, using very small stitches, sew them down.

**4** Trace the hand and heart templates and cut out of felt. Using very small stitches, sew them onto the centre of the brooch front.

**5** Pin and sew the back to the front, leaving the bottom seam open. Stuff, then sew. Sew the clip onto the back 20 mm (¾ in) down from brooch top. Glue on the sequins.

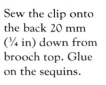

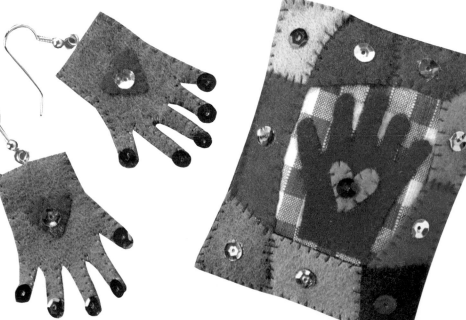

# QUILTING TECHNIQUES

### Tacking for quilting

To achieve good results, the layers of fabric you are working with when quilting – usually top fabric, wadding (batting) and backing fabric – need to be secured together before you begin to stitch. This will prevent the layers from slipping and sliding out of position. To do this, lay the backing fabric wrong side up on a flat, hard surface such as a table and secure it with strips of masking tape at the corners. Lay the other two layers over the top, ending with the top fabric, right side up, and secure them with tape in the same way. Carefully pin the layers together,

working from the centre outwards, remove the masking tape, then work lines of tacking (basting) stitches about 10 cm (4 in) apart both across and down the piece. Begin each row of tacking at the centre using a long length of thread and leave half of it hanging in the middle so you can re-thread your needle to complete the row in the other direction. Remove all the tacking stitches when your quilted design is complete.

For small pieces of quilting, you can use safety pins instead of tacking stitches, but make sure that the pins will not leave visible holes in the fabric when they are removed.

### Quilting by hand

Work the quilting design using small, evenly spaced running stitches. Thread your needle with about 45 cm (18 in) of thread and make a small knot at the long end. Insert the needle into the top fabric a little distance away from the line to be quilted and gently tug the knot through to hide it beneath the fabric.

To finish the thread, make two or three tiny stitches where the row of running stitches ends, then take the needle through the filling and pull the thread through the top fabric a short distance away. Cut off the thread end flush with the surface.

### Applying bias binding

Pin the bias binding on the right side of the fabric with right sides facing and raw edges aligning. Tack (baste) and machine stitch in position with a 6 mm (¼ in) seam allowance. Remove the tacking stitches, turn the free edge of the binding over to the wrong side of the fabric and slip stitch with matching thread to secure in place.

### Quilting by machine

Work a small practice piece before starting to machine quilt to check that your thread, needle, stitch size and fabric are compatible and if necessary adjust these until you achieve the desired result. A 'walking foot' fitted to your machine will help prevent the fabric layers moving and causing puckering. A stitch length of about 8 stitches to 2.5 cm (1 in) works well for quilting, but you may need to alter this to suit the particular fabric you are using. Take time to fit a new needle each time you begin making a project as a blunt one will damage the fabric and cause uneven stitching.

### Slip stitch

Use slip stitch for joining two folded fabric edges together or when securing bias binding. When joining two folds, the stitches are almost invisible and are worked from the right side.

Place the two folded edges together with right sides facing you, slip the needle along inside the fold of one edge, take the needle across to the other edge and slip it along that fold. Pull the thread to draw the edges together.

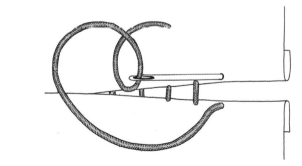

### Running stitch

Use running stitch for hand quilting designs, keeping the stitches small and evenly spaced on both the front and back of the piece.

Work running stitch by passing the needle regularly in and out of the fabric to create the pattern.

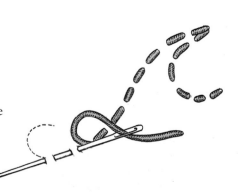

# COT TOY BAG

Early-rising tots will be delighted to find this toy bag hanging at the end of the cot. It is easily made from a furnishing fabric in a design that would appeal to a small child. Here the animal squares have been cut out from a much larger overall pattern, joined and quilted. Measure the width and height of the cot to obtain the bag dimensions.

## YOU WILL NEED
*Furnishing fabric with some eye-catching motifs*
*Scissors*
*Flat wadding (batting)*
*Fabric for bag back*
*Backing muslin (calico)*
*Lining fabric*
*Pins*
*Needle and thread*
*Iron*

**1** Cut out patterns from the furnishing fabric, allowing 6 mm (¼ in) for seams. Cut out one piece of flat wadding (batting), one piece of fabric for the back, one piece of muslin and two pieces of lining to the required size.

**2** Pin, tack and sew the patterned squares together. Press the seams open flat.

**3** Lay the muslin on a flat surface, cover with the wadding (batting) and then the patterned squares, right side up. Pin, then tack the three layers together.

**4** Machine or hand quilt around the animals, neatly knotting the ends of the threads to finish off.

**5** Pin and sew on the backing fabric. Cut loops and binding from the backing fabric 4 cm (1½ in) wide to fit around the top of the bag and make two loops to fit the cot. Fold the loops lengthways and zigzag stitch to neaten the edges. Machine sew the three sides of the bag lining. Join the back and front of the bag, right sides together, and turn through. Drop the lining into the bag and shake down into place. Pin the loops in place and pin the binding around the top of the bag. Sew, then turn the binding to the inside and slip stitch.

# OVEN GLOVE

An oven glove made from a lively fabric is sure to bring a smile to any cook's face. Matching sets of gloves can be made to co-ordinate with the kitchen colour scheme.

## YOU WILL NEED

*Pencil*
*Tracing paper*
*25 cm × 115 cm (¼ yd × 45 in) fabric*
*25 cm × 90 cm (¼ yd × 36 in) thick wadding (batting)*
*25 cm × 115 cm (¼ yd × 45 in) lining fabric*
*Scissors*
*Pins*
*Needle and thread*
*Bias binding for edge and loop*

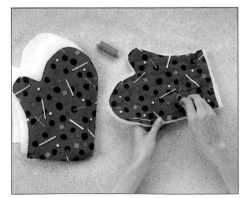

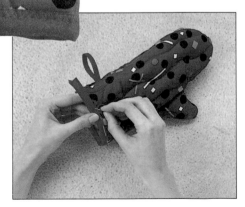

**1** Scale up and trace the templates, then cut out one fabric front, one wadding (batting) and one lining piece for each shape. As the quilting will make the glove shrink a little, leave an extra 12 mm (½ in) seam allowance. Pin and tack together one front, wadding (batting) and lining. Repeat with the other. Quilt in vertical lines.

**2** Place the pattern on the glove and trim neatly leaving 6 mm (¼ in) seam allowance. Make a loop from a strip of bias binding, by folding it in half and sewing the two sides together. Pin the loop to one side of the glove wrist.

**3** Place the two sides of the glove right sides together. Pin, tack and sew. Zigzag around the edges to neaten and turn through. Cut a piece of bias binding slightly larger than the glove wrist. Pin horizontally, then tack and sew in place.

# TISSUE HOLDER

A pretty tissue holder looks attractive on a bedside table or dressing table. This one is small enough to carry around in a little bag or purse.

## YOU WILL NEED
*28 cm (11 in) lace trimming*
*Scissors*
*Pins*
*16.5 cm × 14 cm (6½ in × 5½ in) satin, or to fit small tissue packet*
*16.5 cm × 14 cm (6½ in × 5½ in) cotton lining*
*Needle and thread*
*Iron*
*Packet of tissues*
*Ribbon roses*

**1** Cut the lace into two equal lengths and pin them along the two short sides of the satin on the right side.

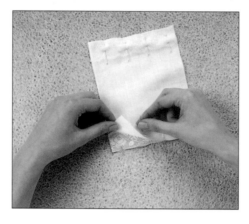

**2** Place the cotton lining on top, pin, tack and sew along the two short sides. Turn through and press.

**3** Mark the centre of each long side with a pinch mark in the fabric, then fold the two short sides inwards to meet in the centre. Machine sew the two open sides. Trim each corner diagonally, zigzag to neaten, then turn through. To finish, insert a packet of tissues and sew pretty ribbon roses at the opening.

# PARTY BIB

The rocking-horse and bird motifs on this little bib make it equally suitable for either a baby boy or a baby girl. Just right for a celebration tea party.

## YOU WILL NEED
Tracing paper
Felt-tip pen
Scissors
30 cm × 115 cm (⅓ yd × 45 in)
    cotton lawn
30 cm (⅓ yd) flat wadding (batting)
Masking tape
Pencil
Pins
Needle and cotton embroidery thread
Bias binding
Button or velcro spots

**1** Draw a bib shape onto tracing paper. Scale up the rocking-horse and bird motif and draw onto tracing paper using a felt-tip pen. Cut out two bib shapes in fabric and one in wadding (batting). Lay the tracing on a white surface and hold in place with masking tape. Centre the bib front over the design and hold the material in place with masking tape. The motif will show through the fabric. Trace the motif onto the bib front using a fine pencil.

**2** Pin together the front, wadding (batting) and back, and tack, working from the centre out, one side at a time.

**3** Quilt over the design with small running stitches.

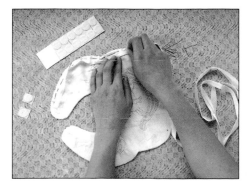

**4** Pin on the bias binding, right sides together, then tack, fold to the back and slip stitch. Make a fastening with either a thread loop and button, or use velcro spots.

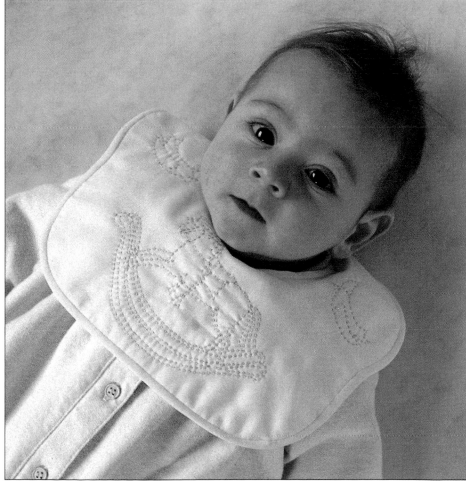

# COSY
# COAT

Quilt tartan fabric, bind with satin and tie a decorative bow to keep your favourite pooch snug on a winter walk. Measure your dog along the back, around the stomach and chest. You could make a trial pattern from some old sheeting instead of paper.

## YOU WILL NEED
Plain paper
Pencil
Scissors
30 cm × 115 cm (⅓ yd × 45 in) tartan fabric
30 cm × 115 cm (⅓ yd × 45 in) wadding (batting)
30 cm × 115 cm (⅓ yd × 45 in) lining
Pins
Needle and thread
Velcro fastenings
Satin bias binding
Satin ribbon

**1** Using the template as a guide, scale up and cut out paper patterns for the right and left sides. Place on the tartan fabric and cut out, making sure that the tartan lines will match across the centre back seam. Cut out the wadding (batting) and lining slightly larger using the pattern as a guide. Pin and tack the top, wadding (batting) and lining together. Quilt along the tartan.

**2** Lay on the patterns once again and trim.

**3** Sew the velcro fastenings on the stomach piece.

**4** Join the two side pieces together along the back. Pin and sew on the bias binding.

**5** Make a bow out of satin ribbon, and sew onto the front together with the velcro fastenings for the chest.

# QUILTED PLACE MATS

A set of place mats adds an elegant touch to a family supper or celebration dinner party. Different fabrics will suit a variety of occasions and the mats can be made from colourful remnants or leftover pieces in the same design as your soft furnishing scheme. The quantities given here are sufficient for four mats, but if you have more fabric, you can make a larger number.

## YOU WILL NEED

4 pieces of interfacing, 33 cm × 28 cm (13 in × 11 in)
4 pieces of plain cotton backing fabric, 37 cm × 32 cm (14½ in × 12½ in)
Pins
Scissors
Needle and thread
4 pieces of patterned cotton fabric, 33 cm × 28 cm (13 in × 11 in)
Masking tape

**1** Pin a piece of the interfacing in the centre of a piece of the backing fabric leaving a border of 20 mm (¾ in) all the way round. Trim the corners of the backing fabric diagonally to allow a neat turnover. Tack (baste) the interfacing in place and remove the pins. Repeat with the remaining pieces of fabric.

**3** Place the patterned fabric pieces on top of the interfacing, leaving an equal border all round. Pin and tack (baste) in place.

**2** Turn over the borders of the backing fabric of each place mat, pin in position and tack (baste) down. To make the corners neat, turn the raw edges under before folding down.

**4** Starting at one corner, lay down a diagonal strip of masking tape as a guideline for the quilting. Tear off a smaller strip of tape and place it next to the first strip. This strip serves as a gauge for the amount of space to be left between the long pieces of tape. Move it along as you lay down these long pieces. Be careful not to overlap the strips as the channel between them is the guide for the stitching. Sew along the edges of the tape. Repeat on the other diagonal to create quilted diamonds. Fold over 12 mm (½ in) of backing fabric, tuck the edge under and sew along the border several times to finish.

# MAKE-UP BAG

This eye-catching make-up bag is made in quilted satin, with a contrasting zip and a co-ordinated lining.

## YOU WILL NEED
25 cm × 115 cm (¼ yd × 45 in) satin
25 cm × 115 cm (¼ yd × 45 in)
   cotton lining
Flat wadding (batting) or flannelette
Scissors
Pins
Needle and thread
20 cm (8 in) zip
Tiny piece of ribbon

**1** Cut out two pieces of satin and lining, each 20 cm × 15 cm (8 in × 6 in), and two pieces of wadding (batting) 20 cm × 14 cm (8 in × 5½ in). Pin and tack together the satin, wadding (batting) and lining, leaving a gap where the wadding (batting) does not reach to the top. This will make it easier to put in the zip.

**2** Quilt by hand or machine. Fold in the top edges of the bag and tack in place.

**3** Lay the zip right side up and place the two folded sides of the bag over it. Pin, tack and sew in place. If you use a machine, attach the zipper foot. Open the zip, then turn the bag through right sides together. Pin, tack and sew around the sides and base edge. Trim then overstitch to neaten. Trim the corners diagonally and turn through to the right side. Tie a tiny piece of ribbon to the zip pull for decoration.

# PADDED COAT HANGER

Padded coat hangers are a must for the well-dressed person, preventing clothes from having hanging marks on the shoulders. These are both decorative and easy to sew. You could also add some pot-pourri in the hanger for a scented gift.

## YOU WILL NEED

*140 cm × 10 cm (55 in × 4 in) wadding (batting) or a double thickness strip the same size as the coat hanger*

*Wooden coat hanger*

*Needle and thread*

*Iron*

*60 cm × 15 cm (24 in × 6 in) strip of fabric*

*Pins*

*Ribbon*

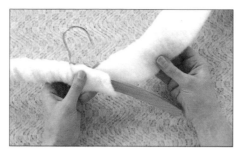

**1** Wind the length of wadding (batting) around the coat hanger, making sure it is even. Sew the ends in place.

**2** Press in a seam allowance of about 6 mm (¼ in) on all four sides of the strip of fabric.

**3** Mark the centre with a pin. Fold the fabric around the hanger with the open edge at the top. Using a double thread, start at one end and sew a running stitch from one end up to the centre. Repeat, starting at the other end.

**4** Gather up each end so that it curves around the hanger. Sew to fasten securely. Wrap the hook in green ribbon and sew in the end.

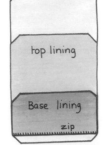

top lining

Base lining

zip

# TRINKET ROLL

A pretty and practical way to store your treasures when on holiday, this roll has two fat 'sausages' for rings and earrings, and a pocket for necklaces and bracelets.

## YOU WILL NEED
*Scissors*
*Ruler*
*30 cm × 115 cm (⅓ yd × 45 in) velvet*
*30 cm × 115 cm (⅓ yd × 45 in) lining*
*Pins*
*Iron*
*Needle and thread*
*18 cm (7 in) zip*
*2.5 m × 15 mm (2¾ yd × ⅝ in) bias binding*
*Small piece of velcro*

**1** Cut out one piece of velvet 33 cm × 23 cm (13 in × 9 in) and round off the four corners. Cut out two pieces of lining 25 cm × 23 cm (10 in × 9 in), and three pieces 23 cm × 11.5 cm (9 in × 4½ in) of velvet. One of these is a pocket and the others are tubes for rings and earrings.

**2** Press in two edges of the lining, centre and place the zip between. Pin and sew in place. Curve the corners to fit the velvet top.

**3** Cut a length of bias binding to fit the velvet pocket and press in half. Fold over the pocket, pin and sew on. Place the pocket on the lining, wrong side up and sew along the bottom. Bring the pocket up and pin the end before tacking (basting) in place.

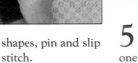

**4** Roll the last two velvet pieces into sausage shapes, pin and slip stitch.

**5** Sew velcro to the end of the one for rings and sew the corresponding piece onto the lining.

**6** Pin the lining onto the wrong side of the velvet, making sure the two sausage shapes are in place. Measure enough bias binding to fit around the edge and leave a length for the ties. Fold the ties in half lengthways and sew. Pin the ties to the centre of one end of the roll. Place the binding, right sides together, on the velvet and pin, then tack (baste) and sew in place. Fold over to the inside and slip stitch. Check that you have caught the edges of the pocket and the 'sausage' for earrings on both sides, but on only one side for the 'sausage' for rings.

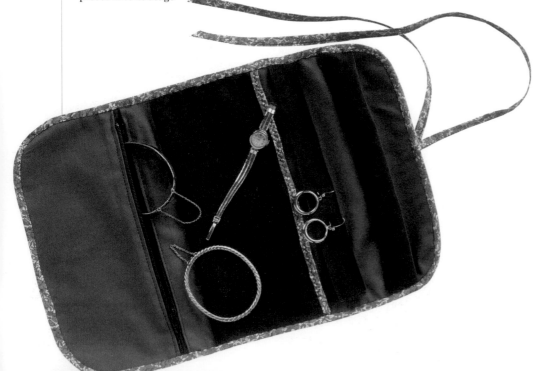

# QUILTED CUSHION COVER

Scraps of furnishing fabric are excellent for making this comfortable quilted cushion cover. The quilting helps it to keep its shape well. The measurements can easily be altered to fit any size of cushion pad; try making an assortment to pile on a comfortable sofa.

## YOU WILL NEED
*Furnishing fabric in two patterns*
*Metal rule*
*Scissors*
*Needle and thread*
*Steam iron*
*45 cm (18 in) square of foam interlining*
*45 cm (18 in) square of backing fabric*
*1 m (1 yd) ribbon*
*41 cm (16 in) cushion pad*

**1** Cut out four squares measuring 15 cm (6 in) and one measuring 23 cm (9 in) of one pattern of furnishing fabric, making sure that the pattern is following the same direction. Cut out two pieces measuring 15 cm (6 in) long and 23 cm (9 in) wide and two pieces measuring 23 cm (9 in) long and 15 cm (6 in) wide of the other pattern of furnishing fabric, again making sure that the pattern is following the same direction. Sew the pieces of fabric together using a 20 mm (¾ in) seam allowance. Press open the seams. Sew the panels together using the same seam allowance and press open.

**2** Lay the cushion front on the interlining, pin together and tack (baste). Machine sew very carefully along each seam line to create a padded appearance.

**4** Make small bows from the ribbon and stitch into place. Push the cushion pad through the opening, making sure the pad is pushed into the corners. Once in position, slipstitch the opening.

**3** With right sides together, pin and tack (baste) the backing fabric to the front. Sew together using a 20 mm (¾ in) seam allowance but leave an opening of about 20 cm (8 in) to enable the cover to be turned through. Trim the corners and seams. Turn through.

### Choosing fabrics for patchwork

Many fabrics are suitable for patchwork, providing they are reasonably firm and do not stretch. A lightweight, pure cotton is probably the best type to use as it will cut and sew well without fraying too badly; patchwork made from cotton can be pressed easily to form crisp flat seams. Use a pure cotton thread for sewing rather than a polyester/cotton blend as this may, in time, wear away the edges of the fabric. When making patchwork avoid furnishing fabrics as these are too thick to handle successfully; knits, stretch fabrics and those with a pile such as velvet are also difficult to use.

### Using templates

When using templates cut from template plastic or card, mark the template with the seam allowance, straight grain and other relevant information. Paper templates do not have the seam allowance included, so you must allow for this when cutting out your patches.

### Straight grain

The term 'straight grain' refers to the fabric threads running from top to bottom in a piece of fabric (the warp) and from side to side (the weft). When cutting out fabric, always align the straight grain marked on your template with the straight grain of the fabric to minimize distortion when joining the patches.

### Using fusible bonding paper

Trace the design elements onto a piece of fusible bonding paper. Cut the paper into separate shapes, then place on the wrong side of your fabric, making sure the adhesive side of the paper is face down. Press in place, setting the iron to the correct temperature for the fabric. Allow to cool, then cut out the shapes (*left*). Lay them in position on the background, adhesive side down, and carefully press with a warm iron.

### Machine stitching

Always work a practice piece before starting to stitch to check that your thread, needle, stitch size and fabric are compatible. Fit a new needle before starting as a blunt one will damage the fabric and may result in uneven stitching.

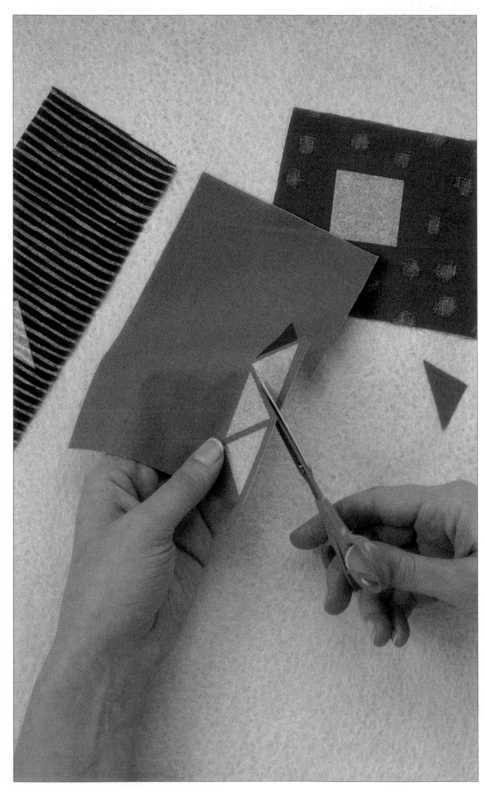

### Applying bias binding

Pin the bias binding on the right side of the fabric with right sides facing and raw edges aligning (*above*). Tack (baste) and stitch in position with a 6 mm (¼ in) seam allowance. Remove the tacking (basting) stitches, turn the free edge of the binding over to the wrong side of the fabric and slip stitch with matching thread to secure in place.

### Whip stitch

Use whip stitch for joining patchwork shapes when they are tacked (basted) over paper templates. Work the stitches evenly and try to keep them as small as possible.

Place two shapes together with right sides together and the edges aligning. Work whip stitch over the two edges, working steadily from right to left.

### Slip stitch

Use slip stitch for joining two folded fabric edges together or when securing bias binding. When joining two folds, the stitches are almost invisible and are worked from the right side. Place the two folded edges together with right sides facing you, slip the needle along inside the fold of one edge, take the needle across to the other edge and slip it along that fold.

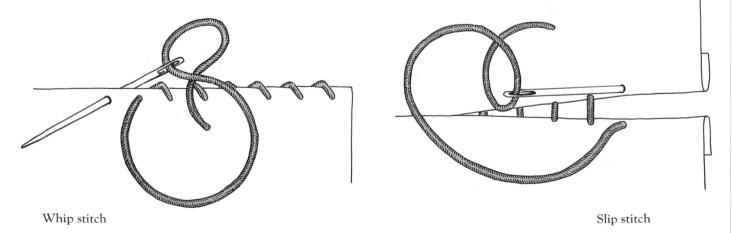

Whip stitch

Slip stitch

# NOTICE BOARD

Postcards, messages and lists can be displayed on this colourful cheerful patchwork notice board. It is easily made and is light enough to be hung using self-adhesive velcro spots.

**1** Cut out four 16.5 cm (6½ in) squares from each of the four colours of fabric.

**2** Lay out the squares in the chosen order. Sew the squares together first in pairs, then in fours, and finally in rows. Check the squares and press after each addition.

**3** When all the squares are joined, measure two opposite sides and cut out a 10 cm (4 in) wide piece of

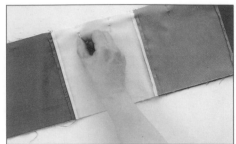

black fabric to fit. Pin and sew, then press. Repeat for the remaining two sides. Press well.

**4** Stick the velcro spots in place on the polystyrene. Lay the patchwork wrong side up on a flat surface. Place the polystyrene board over it, centring over the patches. Wrap the black bands around, holding in place with map pins. Fold the corners neatly and secure with more map pins.

**5** On the right side, pin lengths of black ribbon, folding under the ends, to form a diamond lattice design. Where they cross each other, secure with drawing pins (thumb tacks).

# SUFFOLK PUFF EARRINGS

Handmade earrings are always interesting, and the Suffolk Puff patchwork technique lends itself well to these beaded silk beauties.

## YOU WILL NEED
Card
Pair of compasses
Pencil
Pair of felt-covered earring bases
15 cm × 7.5 cm (6 in × 3 in) green silk
Fray check liquid
Scissors
Needle and thread
Tiny piece of pink satin
Pink beads

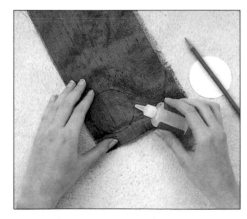

**1** Make a circular template in card twice the size of the earring base and draw around it onto the green silk. Apply fray check liquid over this line. When it is dry, cut out the fabric.

**2** Turn in a narrow hem and run a gathering stitch around the circle.

**3** Draw up the gathering stitch thread, so that the circle puffs, insert a small piece of satin into the centre, then tie a knot to finish off. Slip stitch the puff onto the earring base, making sure it is in the centre.

**4** Sew tiny beads all along the edge. Repeat the steps to make the other earring.

# SCENTED SACHETS

These little patchwork sachets are made to appear gift-wrapped by using the Seminole patchwork technique. They are quick to make in batches of six. Filled with pot-pourri they give a delicate fragrance when tucked into drawers.

## YOU WILL NEED

25 cm × 115 cm (¼ yd × 45 in) *patterned fabric (to make 6 sachets)*

25 cm × 115 cm (¼ yd × 45 in) *plain fabric (to make 6 sachets)*

*Scissors*

*Pins*

*Needle and thread*

*Iron*

*Patchwork square rule or set (T) square*

*Pot-pourri*

*Wadding (batting)*

*Pinking shears*

**1** Cut out two strips 45 cm × 6.5 cm (18 in × 2½ in) of the patterned fabric and three strips 45 cm × 2.5 cm (18 in × 1 in) of the plain fabric. Cut out six pieces 12.5 cm × 7.5 cm (5 in × 3 in) of the plain fabric for the backing. Sew the two wide strips on either side of one of the narrow strips, and press seams open flat.

**2** Straighten the ends with a patchwork square rule or set square to make each sachet. Measure and cut out two 4 cm (1½ in) strips down the joined strip.

**3** Cut out a 12.5 cm (5 in) piece from one of the plain fabric strips. Pin, then sew this between the two joined strips, so that a cross of plain fabric is made. Press.

**4** Place the backing piece and front right sides together, pin and sew around three sides of the sachet. Trim the corners diagonally, then turn through and press.

**5** Fill the sachet with pot-pourri and wadding (batting). Slip stitch to close. Using pinking shears, cut a narrow strip of the plain fabric, tie into a bow and sew on top.

# PIN CUSHION

Triangles of black and white striped fabric are joined together to make this hexagonal pin cushion with an effective chevron design. This simple technique is known as English patchwork. Spotted fabric has been used on the back.

## YOU WILL NEED
*Pencil*
*Template plastic or card*
*Scissors*
*Stiff paper*
*30 cm × 10 cm (12 in × 4 in) striped fabric*
*30 cm × 10 cm (12 in × 4 in) spotted fabric*
*Pins*
*Needle and thread*
*Iron*
*Wadding (batting)*

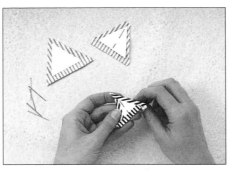

**2** Fold one of the paper templates in half, open and place on the wrong side of one of the striped triangles. Make sure the folded line runs along a stripe. Pin, then fold over the seam allowance and tack (baste) through the paper. Continue until you have six striped and six spotted pieces.

**3** To join the triangles, place the triangles right sides together and match up the stripes. Using a small fine needle, whip stitch the triangles together until you have made two hexagons. Press.

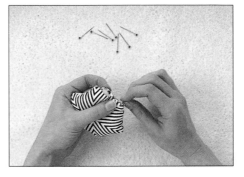

**4** Place the hexagons right sides together and whip stitch around the edge, leaving a gap for stuffing.

Gently snip the tacking stitches and remove the papers. Turn through and stuff with wadding (batting) until firm.

**5** Slip stitch to close.

**1** Draw an equilateral triangle onto template plastic or card and cut out. Check that the triangle is accurate by placing it on paper and drawing round it once, then turning it around to make sure it fits whichever way it is placed. There is no seam allowance. Draw around the pattern 12 times onto stiff paper and cut out the triangles. Draw around the template six times onto the wrong side of the striped fabric and six times onto the spotted fabric, allowing 6 mm (¼ in) seam allowance between each triangle. Make sure that one stripe runs from the top point to the base of each triangle. Cut out.

# PEG BAG

Hanging out your washing on the line is easier if the clothes pegs are kept in a special bag. A rotary cutter and self-heal mat help to ensure the quick and accurate cutting of fabric for patchwork.

## YOU WILL NEED
Saw
Wooden coat hanger
Tape measure
Rotary cutter or scissors
30 cm × 115 cm (⅓ yd × 45 in) patterned fabric
25 cm × 115 cm (¼ yd × 45 in) contrasting plain fabric
50 cm × 115 cm (½ yd × 45 in) lining
Needle and thread
Steam iron
Pair of compasses
Pencil
Ruler
Tracing paper
Pins
Bias binding

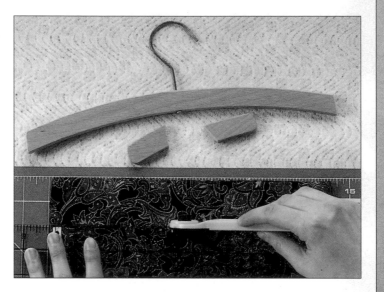

**1** Using a saw, cut off the ends of the coat hanger so that it measures 33 cm (13 in). Cut out five strips measuring 70 cm × 5 cm (28 in × 2 in) of the patterned fabric and four identical strips of the plain fabric. Cut out a 70 cm × 35 cm (28 in × 13½ in) piece of lining.

**2** Sew the strips in pairs with a 6 mm (¼ in) seam allowance until all nine are joined. Press the seams open. Trim the ends straight.

**3** Draw a 15 cm (6 in) diameter circle on tracing paper and cut out. Place the lining right side down and the joined strips right side up on top. Place the template 7.5 cm (3 in) from the top and equidistant from the sides. Pin the two layers of fabric around the circle to stop them from moving, then draw around the template in pencil. Cut out the circle.

**4** Measure the circumference of the circle and cut a piece of bias binding slightly larger. Join with a diagonal seam.

**5** Pin, tack and sew the bias binding in place.

**6** Fold the fabric in half right sides together, keeping the circular opening at the top. Place the coat hanger at the top and mark the curve of the hanger using a pencil. Cut just outside this line leaving about 6 mm (¼ in) seam allowance. Pin the three sides and sew, leaving a gap for the hook at the top. Trim the corners diagonally. Zigzag stitch around to neaten the seams. Turn through and insert the coat hanger.

# HEART WALLHANGING

This striking design is made very economically from small pieces of calico, each appliquéd with a different patterned fabric heart. The pieces are sewn together to make a complete picture, and then finished off with a fabric border.

## YOU WILL NEED
*Drawing paper*
*Pencil*
*Scissors*
*Pins*
*Remnants of patterned fabric*
*Pieces of calico*
*Steam iron*
*Needle and thread*

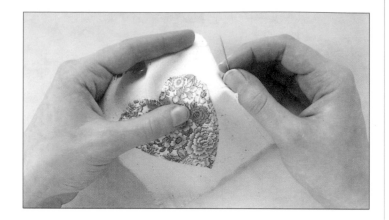

**1** Make a heart-shaped template and pin onto a scrap of printed fabric. Draw round the template and cut out adding a border of 6 mm (¼ in) all the way round for the seam allowance. Repeat with the other scraps of patterned fabric. Cut out large enough rectangles of calico for the hearts to have a surrounding border. Press each fabric piece flat and then turn the seam allowance under. Pin each heart shape onto a calico rectangle and sew into position using either an overcast or running stitch.

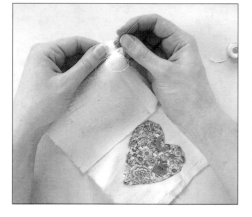

**2** Arrange the pieces in a pleasing pattern and sew the rectangles together in rows turning the edges under. Cut a bias strip of patterned fabric about 5 cm (2 in) wide for the border and sew into place.

# COT QUILT

This original cot quilt with colourful patchwork blocks and binding would make a beautiful gift for a new-born baby. You could add a label embroidered with the baby's name and date of birth.

## YOU WILL NEED

1.5 m × 115 cm (1½ yd × 45 in) *spotted fabric*

25 cm (¼ yd) each of 4 contrasting *fabrics*

70 cm × 90 cm (¾ yd × 36 in) *wadding (batting)*

70 cm × 115 cm (¾ yd × 45 in) *backing fabric*

*Ruler*

*Rotary mat and cutter or scissors*

*Pins*

*Needle and thread*

*Iron*

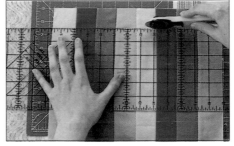

**1** Cut out two lengths 90 cm × 14 cm (36 in × 5½ in), four lengths 40 cm × 14 cm (15½ in × 5½ in) and three squares 14 cm (5½ in) of the spotted fabric. Using the template, cut out six triangles from each of the contrasting fabrics and 24 from the spotted fabric. The template and measurements include a 6 mm (¼ in) seam allowance. Join the contrasting fabric triangles together to form squares, first pinning then sewing, checking and pressing before each stage. Add a spotted triangle on each side of these squares to form diamond shapes.

**2** Join the three spotted squares to the patched squares, so there is a spotted square on either side. This forms the centre strip. Next join two patched squares at either end of one of the shorter lengths of spotted fabric. Repeat so that these two lengths fit either side of the centre strip, with the three spotted squares. Join them together and press. Join the two remaining medium spotted strips to the top and bottom of the quilt centre. Finally join the two long spotted strips on either side of the quilt. The quilt should now measure 90 cm × 65 cm (36 in × 25½ in).

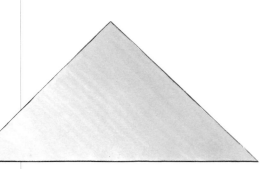

**3** Tack together the top, wadding (batting) and backing fabric. Machine or hand quilt, making sure that the quilting lines are no further than 10 cm (4 in) apart. Trim the edges neatly.

**4** To make the binding, cut two 45 cm × 5 cm (18 in × 2 in) strips of each contrasting colour fabric, and join them together to make a piece 45 cm × 32 cm (18 in × 12 in). Cut across these strips as shown, then join to make the binding, about 300 cm (120 in) long.

**5** Pin the binding in place at the top and bottom with the right sides together, and sew. Attach the binding to the sides in the same way. Fold over to the back and slip stitch in place.

# FESTIVE TABLE MAT

This festive table mat can be used year after year until it becomes a family heirloom. It could also be used as a wall hanging. The design is based on two squares which rotate to form triangles. The larger of the triangles are strip-patched with Christmassy co-ordinating fabrics. A rotary cutter and self-healing board speed up cutting strip patches.

## YOU WILL NEED
*Pencil*
*Template plastic*
*Craft knife or rotary cutter*
*Ruler*
*Scissors*
*Assorted festive and co-ordinating fabrics*
*Pins*
*Needle and thread*
*Steam iron*
*Heavy vilene*

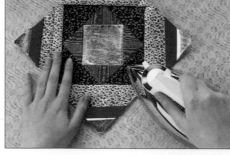

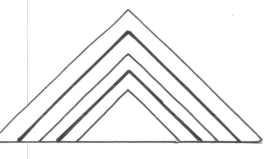

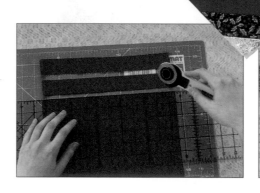

**1** Scale up and trace the templates onto plastic. There is no seam allowance so draw round them and use the edges as a stitching guide. Cut out strips of fabric 4 cm (1½ in) wide. The larger triangles will require six strips, the smaller four.

**2** Pin, tack (baste) and sew the strips in pairs, right sides together, chain-style, leaving a seam allowance of 6 mm (¼ in). Press the seams flat and join in pairs again to produce a large striped panel.

**3** Place the templates on the back of the joined strips and cut out leaving a seam allowance of 6 mm (¼ in) between each triangle.

**4** Working from the centre out join on all the components, including the central square and triangles. Press between each addition.

**5** When the mat is completed, cut a piece of vilene to fit. Turn the seam allowance over and slip stitch into place. A further backing may be sewn on if you wish.

# GREETINGS CARD

Needle and thread are not necessary for making this ingenious patchwork greetings card. As only very small pieces of fabric are needed, many combinations can be achieved by merely using scraps.

## YOU WILL NEED
*Pencil*
*Fusible iron-on bonding paper*
*Three-fold greetings card with cut-out aperture*
*Steam iron*
*Small pieces of three contrasting fabrics*
*Narrow double-sided tape*

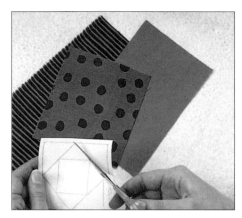

**1** Draw your patchwork design onto fusible bonding paper. Making sure the three-fold card is the right way up, outline the square in pencil as a guide.

**2** Cut up the bonding paper and place the pieces of the design in separate heaps. Using a steam iron, press the shapes onto the reverse side of the chosen contrasting fabrics.

**3** Cut out the shapes carefully and peel off the backing paper from all the pieces. Arrange them within the square on the card to form a block. Press gently with a warm steam iron.

**4** Put double-sided tape around the aperture and the card edges, then peel off the backing paper. Close the card carefully, smoothing from the folded side outwards.

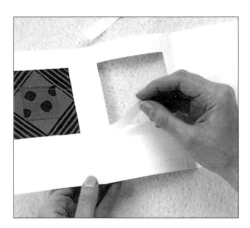

# PATCHWORK CUSHION

This striking design is surprisingly quick to make, using just one template. Experiment with placing the strips of triangles in different combinations.

## YOU WILL NEED
*Template plastic*
*Pencil*
*Ruler*
*Pieces of black and white fabrics, each about 36 cm × 18 cm (14 in × 7 in)*
*White pencil*
*Scissors*
*Pins*
*Patchwork square rule*
*25 cm × 115 cm (¼ yd × 45 in) turquoise fabric*
*25 cm × 115 cm (¼ yd × 45 in) blue fabric*
*Needle and thread*
*Iron*
*164 cm (64 in) strip of striped fabric*
*38 cm (15 in) cushion pad*

1 Using the template as a guide and including 6 mm (¼ in) seam allowance, draw 20 triangles on the black fabric and 20 on the white, having first drawn two parallel lines along the grain of each fabric in which to fit the triangles.

2 Cut out and pin the triangles in pairs of one black and one white, keeping the straight grain along the top and bottom. Continue to pin pairs until you have four strips of five pairs. Each alternate strip should start with a white triangle and finish with a black one.

3 Pin the strips together, offsetting the black points to the centre of the black triangle in the next row.

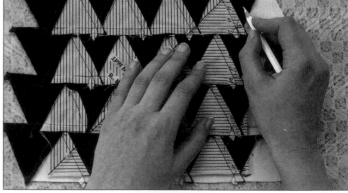

4 Using a patchwork square rule draw a 20 cm (8 in) square plus 6 mm (¼ in) seam allowance on the wrong side, centred so that the points of the triangles balance. These lines will be your stitching lines. Trim to 6 mm (¼ in) seam allowance.

**5** Measure opposite sides of the square and cut two strips of turquoise fabric 9 cm (3½ in) wide to fit. Pin with right sides together, sew and press flat. Measure remaining sides and cut two strips of blue fabric 9 cm (3½ in) wide to fit. Pin with right sides together, sew and press flat.

**6** Continue in the same manner, cutting black and white striped fabric 3 cm (1¼ in) wide to fit. Pin, sew and press. To make the back of the cover, cut a piece of blue fabric to fit the width plus 6 mm (¼ in) seam allowance. Cut a piece of turquoise fabric of the same width but longer for the overlap. Turn in a hem at one end of each piece. Place the two pieces, right sides together, over the patchwork square. Pin, sew and snip off the corners diagonally, so that the corners will be sharp. Invert and press. Insert the cushion pad.

# PAINTED SILK SCARF

Freehand painting on silk gives a beautiful effect as the colours merge and shine on the fabric. Experiment with designs to suit favourite outfits, or paint matching ones for a family group. Silk paints can be found in most craft or art supply shops.

## YOU WILL NEED
*Hemmed natural silk square*
*Pins*
*Old picture frame*
*Pen*
*Paper*
*Silk outliner (gutta)*
*Non-toxic silk dyes in an assortment*
   *of colours*
*Soft paintbrushes*
*Sponge*
*Iron*

**1** Stretch the silk square by pinning it onto an old picture frame. Sketch out your design on paper, and draw the outline onto the silk using the silk outliner (gutta). This prevents the colours from running.

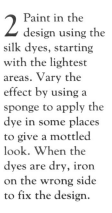

**2** Paint in the design using the silk dyes, starting with the lightest areas. Vary the effect by using a sponge to apply the dye in some places to give a mottled look. When the dyes are dry, iron on the wrong side to fix the design.

# PRESERVE JAR COVERS

Homemade preserves are a delight on any breakfast table and look even more tempting with these traditional cotton covers. The design can be adapted according to the type of preserve: try oranges, raspberries or blueberries, as well as that old favourite – strawberries.

## YOU WILL NEED
*Plate*
*Pencil*
*Remnants of gingham or printed cotton*
*Pinking shears*
*Scissors*
*Coloured felt*
*Rubber-based adhesive*
*Black fabric pen*
*Elastic band*
*Narrow red ribbon*

**1** Using a plate about 7.5 cm (3 in) wider than the jar lid, draw a circle on the wrong side of the fabric. Cut out using pinking shears. Cut out strawberry shapes and green leaves from the felt.

**2** Stick the strawberries and leaves onto the central area of the fabric using rubber-based adhesive.

**3** Carefully mark the pips on the fruit using a black fabric pen.

**4** Place the cover on the jar and secure with an elastic band. Finish by tying a piece of red ribbon into a neat bow.

# T-SHIRT

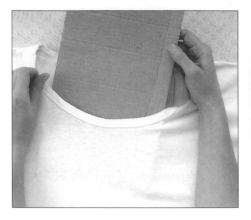

Give your plain white T-shirt a new lease of life with this striking tulip design. Why not wear your art on your sleeve, chest or back?

YOU WILL NEED
*White T-shirt*
*Steam iron*
*Piece of cardboard*
*Green, red and brown fabric paints*
*Small paintbrush*

**1** Iron the T-shirt and slip a piece of cardboard inside it so that the paint will not seep through to the back. Make sure the T-shirt is quite flat by smoothing it out with your hands.

**2** Start the design using green fabric paints, painting the green stalks first. Next paint the red tulips, extending them slightly around the neck to emphasize the shape. Draw an outline of brown fabric paint with the brush to enhance and define the design. Iron the T-shirt to fix the fabric paint.

# HAIR SCRUNCHY

Scraps of pretty fabric can be used to make hair ornaments. Try to match a special outfit for a party or birthday outing.

## YOU WILL NEED
*20 cm × 14 cm (8 in × 5½ in) satin*
*    fabric*
*Pins*
*Needle and thread*
*15 cm (6 in) narrow elastic*

**1** With the right sides together, fold the fabric in half lengthways. Pin together, allowing 10 mm (⅜ in) for the seam, and stitch.

**2** Press the seam open and turn through to the right side.

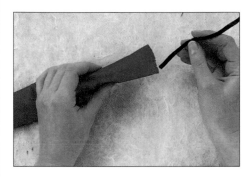

**3** Thread the elastic through the fabric tube and stitch one end securely.

**4** Gather the fabric along the length of the elastic until it forms a 'scrunched' shape.

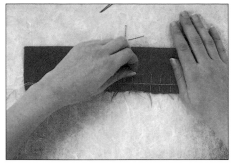

**5** Turn under 10 mm (⅜ in) of fabric at one end. Sew together the ends of the elastic and slip stitch the ends of the fabric together securely.

# FANCY HAIRBAND

This fancy hairband is guaranteed to attract compliments and could be made to match any outfit. Experiment with other interesting trimmings which could also be used to decorate a simple fabric hairband.

## YOU WILL NEED

48 cm × 16 cm (19 in × 6½ in) fabric
Pins
Needle and thread
Tape measure
Steam iron
1 m (1 yd) pompon braid
16 cm (6½ in) elastic, 15 mm (⅝ in) wide

**1** Fold the rectangle of fabric in half lengthways, right sides together. Pin and sew the long edges together, and turn through.

**2** Turn the unfinished ends in 12 mm (½ in). Press flat with the seam in the centre of the underside of the hairband.

**3** Place the hairband top side up and pin the braid down both sides with the pompons facing outwards. Sew the braid in place and secure the ends firmly.

**4** Run a gathering thread around one open end of the hairband. Place one end of the elastic into the centre of the open end and draw up the gathering thread around it. Sew the gathered end and the elastic firmly in place. Check the hairband for size and repeat with the other end.

# A FLORAL TOUCH

Add a delicate and decorative motif to an old pillowcase using fabric pens. If you like, create a matching set by using the same motif on some sheets. Fabric pens are now easily available in all craft shops and can be used to add a personal touch to cotton or silk. Once the design is finished the fabric can be washed and pressed in the normal way.

### YOU WILL NEED
*Clean cotton or silk pillowcase*
*Steam iron*
*Heavy cardboard*
*Fabric pens in an assortment of*
 *colours*
*Clean cloth*

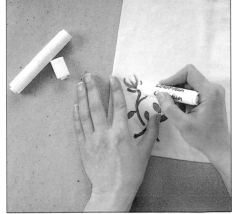

**1** Press the pillowcase to remove any creases. Insert a piece of heavy cardboard inside the pillowcase to protect the fabric on the other side from any ink that may leak through. Hold the fabric taut and smooth and apply the first colour of the motif.

**2** Keep the fabric smooth and continue to build up the design by applying the second colour.

**3** Fill in the detail by adding more colours until the design is complete. To fix the colours, cover with a clean cloth and press with a hot iron for 1-2 minutes, taking care not to leave the iron in one place for more than a few seconds.

# WILD BEAST NAPKIN RINGS

Give your dinner guests something to talk about by making these unusual felt napkin rings. Not only do these wild beasts look good chasing their tails around a napkin, but when everyone unwraps their napkins, the beasts will look great racing each other around the table!

## YOU WILL NEED
*For each napkin ring:*
*Pencil*
*Thin card*
*Scissors*
*18 cm × 14 cm (7 in × 5½ in)*
*   coloured felt*
*Small amounts of black and white felt*
*Needle and thread*
*Small press-stud (snap fastener)*

**1** Draw an animal shape on thin card. Cut out and place it on the coloured felt. Draw around the shape and cut out the animal.

**2** Cut out a small white felt circle and a smaller black felt circle for the eye, and sew into place.

**3** Sew the press-stud (snap fastener) halves in place on the nose and bottom of the animals. Fasten around the napkin.

# CUSTOMIZED SHOES

Use fabric pens for a great way of brightening up a pair of inexpensive fabric shoes and giving them a 'designer' look.

## YOU WILL NEED
*Pair of fabric shoes in a plain colour*
*Newspaper*
*Fabric pens with fine and thick tips*
*Assorted glitter inks and expanding fabric paints*

**1** Stuff the shoes with newspaper. Draw zigzags on the sides of the shoes, and some pink spirals all over the front of the shoes.

**2** Using silver glitter ink, add zigzags and dots.

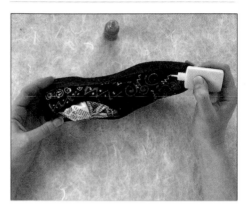

**3** Dot around the edges of the shoes with expanding fabric paint. Leave to dry.

# MILLION-DOLLAR HAT

Buy lots of inexpensive ribbon and ready-made rosebuds and make an old straw hat look like a million dollars for a special occasion.

## YOU WILL NEED
*Assortment of wide and narrow satin*
*ribbons*
*Scissors*
*Straw hat*
*Strong clear glue*
*Needle and wide thread*
*Satin ribbon rosebuds*

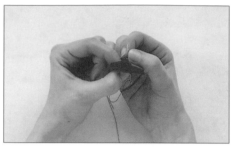

**1** Cut a long piece of wide ribbon for the main band. Cut long pieces of narrow ribbon to place around the hat and shorter pieces of wide ribbon to make rosebuds. Glue the long piece of ribbon around the hat.

**2** Using a shorter piece of wide ribbon, start at one end and roll it loosely until it forms a coil. Then gripping the coil at the bottom, sew it together to secure the shape of a rosebud.

**3** For the leaf, fold a shorter piece of wide green ribbon, so that the two ends meet halfway across the middle. Stick this seam together with glue. Place the rosebuds over the seams on the leaf and glue them together. Leave to dry, then secure even further with one or two stitches. Make as many rose-buds as you require in lots of different colours and sizes.

**4** Place the rosebud stems mainly at the back of the hat in a cluster to hide the meeting points of the ribbon glued around the hat. Then place the little ready-made rosebuds around the brim of the hat in a semi-ordered fashion. Secure these with one or two little stitches through the straw of the hat.

# TIE-DYED SCARF

The technique of tie-dying is very simple to master. You can easily produce stunning artistic effects by altering the pattern of knots and colours.

## YOU WILL NEED

*Needle and thread*
*Pre-hemmed square of natural white silk*
*Scissors*
*Cotton string or raffia*
*Rubber gloves*
*Cold or hot dyes, in 2 colours*
*Bucket or stainless steel pan*
*Spoon for stirring*

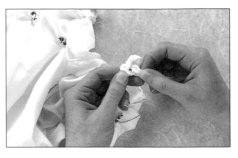

**1** Pass the needle and thread through the silk square, and pull and twist the thread around tightly until you have a tight little 'peak' at least 20 mm (¾ in) long. Knot the thread and cut the end. Make at least 15 little peaks in the same way, scattered over the scarf.

**2** Fold the silk over into a triangle, and make two tight knots at each corner.

**3** Fold over once more to form a smaller triangle. Hold the fabric in the centre and bring the two ends to- gether. Criss-cross the string over the silk until you almost reach the knotted corners. Tie the string securely.

**4** Wearing rubber gloves, prepare the first dye in a bucket or stainless steel pan following the manufacturer's instructions. When the dye is ready for use, immerse the knotted silk scarf stirring occasionally. Cold dyes require 60 minutes, hot dyes 10–15 minutes. Then remove the scarf and rinse it under cold water until this runs clear.

**5** Untie the cord binding and the knots at the corners of the silk. Unfold the scarf, leaving the little peaks. Refold in the opposite direction so that the corners of the triangle which were double become single and vice versa. Knot each corner three times. Holding the middle of the longest side, twist and knot two or three times until you reach the knotted corners of the scarf.

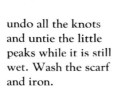

**6** Prepare the second dye as before and proceed in the same way. When the silk is thoroughly rinsed, undo all the knots and untie the little peaks while it is still wet. Wash the scarf and iron.

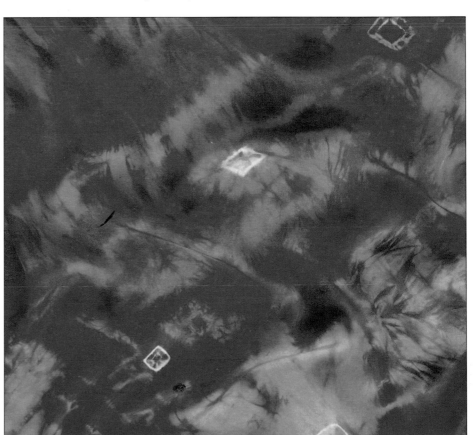

# KNOTTED HAIRBAND

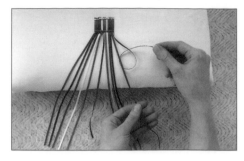

You can make this unusual hairband with a variety of coloured ribbons, and even produce a series to co-ordinate with different outfits or for special occasions.

## YOU WILL NEED

*Pins*
*Cushion pad*
*2 m (2 yd) lengths of 3 mm (⅛ in)*
*wide ribbons in 6 colours*
*Wide elastic*
*Needle and thread*

**1** Starting with two ribbons of the same colour in the middle, pin the ribbons on the cushion pad. Pin the other ribbons to the left and right of the central pair so that the colours on the left reflect those on the right. Place another row of pins 2.5 cm (1 in) down from the first row. Following diagram 1, begin knotting with the first ribbon on the left, working across to the right until you reach the centre point.

**3** Next divide the 12 ribbons into four groups of three. Braid in the conventional way to produce four braids 4 cm (1½ in) long.

**2** Now knot from the first ribbon on the right side following the knotting technique shown in diagram 2. Continue knotting from both sides to the centre for 14 rows.

**4** Divide the braids into two bunches and wrap one bunch tightly with one of the ribbons. Repeat with the other bunch. Swop the colours and continue wrapping for 5 cm (2 in). Divide the ribbons again into braiding groups and continue braiding and wrapping until you have the desired length.

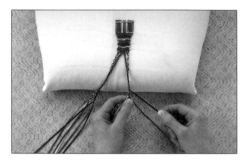

**5** Pin and knot the ends of the ribbons and cut off any excess.

**6** Stitch a short length of wide elastic to the ribbon knots, passing the thread through the knots to secure.

# RIBBON
# WREATH

This charming variation on the traditional festive wreath is perfect for hanging on a room door or on the wall. It is not suitable for a front door as rain would spoil the paper.

## YOU WILL NEED

2 lengths of red paper ribbon, 8 cm (3¼ in) wide
Scissors
Roll of green crepe paper 2.5 m (2½ yd) long
Reel of copper wire
Wire cutters
Strong clear glue
2 m × 12 mm (2 yd × ½ in) gold ribbon
Awl
2 m × 12 mm (2 yd × ½ in) green ribbon
2 m × 20 mm (2 yd × ¾ in) red satin ribbon
2 m × 20 mm (2 yd × ¾ in) green satin ribbon
Artificial red berries mounted on wire

**1** Concertina one length of the red paper ribbon into 7 cm (2¾ in) folds. With the ribbon folded cut zig-zag shapes at the top and bottom.

Cut a long strip of green crepe paper 20 cm (8 in) wide. Fold in half lengthways and cut out feathery shapes 5 cm (2 in) deep on the top and bottom.

**2** Unfold the red paper ribbon. Lay the copper wire along the centre lengthways and cut the wire to this length. Draw a line of glue along the centre of the red

paper ribbon. Place the copper wire on this. Cut a matching length of gold ribbon and stick over the copper wire, making sure it also sticks to the red paper.

**3** Unfold the green crepe paper and line it with the second length of red paper ribbon. Lay on a flat surface with the red uppermost, and place the red paper strip with the gold ribbon at right

angles on top. Hold down firmly. Fold the green crepe paper strip over the red paper strip at right angles. Repeat this process in the opposite direction until the strips are completely over each other.

**4** Hold the folded paper together and using an awl, pierce two holes 2.5 cm (1 in) apart in the centre, piercing through all the layers at once. Twist two strands of copper wire together to make 2

× 60 cm (2 ft) lengths of stronger wire. Thread the twisted wire strands through the holes and fasten the ends together to form a circle. Open the concertina gently to create a wreath.

**5** Decorate by twisting berries and ribbons over

and under the gaps, using the wires to hold them in place.

# CHRISTMAS BALLET SHOES

Transform a pair of ballet shoes to wear at a Christmas party by decorating them with brightly coloured berries and ribbons. For this pair, ribbon with a floating thread at the back was gathered up the centre.

## YOU WILL NEED
*Pair of ballet shoes*
*Artificial holly berries*
*Needle and thread*
*20 cm (8 in) narrow metallic ribbon*
*Ribbon with floating thread, four*
*times the length of each shoe*

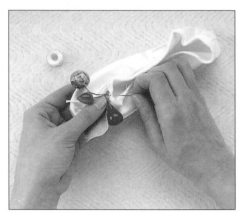

**1** For each shoe, bind some berries together, and sew onto the fronts of the shoes.

**2** Cut the length of metallic ribbon in half. Form three loops in each piece, with the largest loop at the bottom. Sew the loops over the berries.

**3** Gather the ribbon to fit round each shoe by pulling on the floating thread.

**4** Sew the ribbon in position around the top of the shoe. Finish with a twirl at the front to cover and obscure the points where the loops and berries join the shoe.

# HAIR CLIP

Disguise a plain hair clip with a pretty ribbon bow to match your dress.

## YOU WILL NEED
*21 cm (8½ in) length of ribbon*
*6 cm (2¼ in) length of ribbon*
*Needle and thread*
*Plain hair clip*

**1** Fold the ends of the longer piece of ribbon inwards to meet in the centre and sew them together. Leave the thread long.

**2** Pull on the thread to gather the join.

**3** Wrap the shorter piece of ribbon over the join.

**4** Sew the ends together at the back and sew the bow onto the clip.

# ROSETTE EARRINGS

These unusual clip-on earrings, quickly made with coiled ribbon, can also be used to decorate a pair of shoes.

## YOU WILL NEED
*1 m (1 yd) wide ribbon*
*Needle and thread*
*Pair of clip-on earring backs*

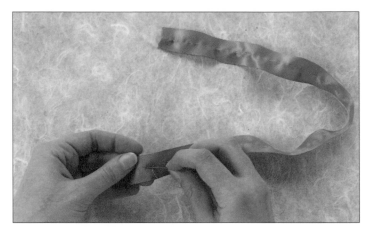

**1** Cut the length of ribbon in half and use one piece for each earring. Sew a line of running stitches down the centre of the ribbon.

**2** Gather the stitches up evenly and coil the ribbon around itself. Secure the coil with a few running stitches.

**3** Sew the coil onto the back of each earring.

# RIBBON PURSE

This ribbon creation uses simple techniques practised by weavers over the centuries. By interlacing lengths of silk ribbon you can make a pretty purse in no time.

## YOU WILL NEED

*Double-sided tape*
*Empty tissue box*
*Assortment of coloured silk ribbons including black, of different widths, each 1.5 m (60 in) long*
*Tapestry needle*
*Small rectangle of self-adhesive black felt*
*Tailor's chalk*
*Scissors*
*Pins*
*Small rectangle of black cotton satin*
*Needle and thread*
*2 black glass buttons*
*Short length of round black elastic*

**1** Stick double-sided tape all around the upper part on the sides of the box. Peel off the protective backing. Fix one end of a length of ribbon onto the tape and cross the ribbon over to the other side of the box. Stretch it lightly, fix the end onto the tape and trim. Repeat until the whole box is covered, taking care that the pieces do not overlap. The weft is now ready.

**2** Thread a tapestry needle with a length of ribbon. Pass the needle alternately under and over each ribbon of the weft, to the opposite side. Fix the ribbon onto the tape and cut off the remaining ribbon. It might be necessary to push each row of the warp against the previous one with your fingers to get the best results. Repeat to the end.

**3** Invert the tissue box and place on the self-adhesive felt. Draw round with tailor's chalk and cut out.

**4** Peel off the protective backing and apply sticky-side down onto the ribbons. Press down firmly. Using scissors cut off all the ribbons right round the sides of the box. Trim.

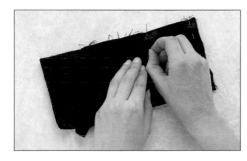

**5** Pin the piece of black satin onto the felt, wrong side down. Sew the edges to the felt. Turn inside out.

**6** Fold the remaining black ribbon in half lengthways and tack (baste) around the purse. Fold the purse in three. Sew the two sides together and sew the ribbon around. Sew on a glass button at each corner of the over-lap. Sew on two loops of elastic.

# FRILLY SOCKS

Transform a pair of white socks with frilled ribbon for a little girl to wear to a party.

## YOU WILL NEED
2.5 m × 15 mm (2¾ yd × ⅝ in) narrow ribbon
Scissors
Needle and thread
Pins
Pair of plain socks

**1** Cut the ribbon into six equal lengths. Sew a line of running stitches as near to one edge as possible of each piece of ribbon.

**2** Pull the ribbon up the thread to gather the length of ribbon. Repeat with the other pieces of ribbon.

**3** Starting at the back, pin the gathered edge of the ribbon to the top of the sock to hold it in place. When you have pinned the ribbon all the way round, make sure both ends overlap slightly.

**4** Tack the ribbon in place and then secure it with a line of backstitch, stretching the sock as you work, so it will still fit over the child's ankle.

**5** Sew on the other two lengths at 10 mm (⅜ in) intervals. Repeat with the other sock.

# GIANT BOW

Make a giant bow to trim a gift-wrapped package. Choose colours that tone with the paper or make a good contrast.

## YOU WILL NEED
*2 m (2 yd) lengths of twisted paper*
*rope in 2 different colours*
*2 m (2 yd) satin ribbon*
*Sticky tape*

**1** Untwist the lengths of coloured paper rope and spread them out.

**2** Twist the paper rope strands together with the satin ribbon.

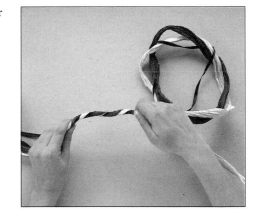

**3** Wrap around the middle of a gift-wrapped package and tie the remaining loose untwisted ends into a bow. Use a small piece of sticky tape to fasten in place if necessary.

# RIBBON DECORATIONS

There are many different effects that can be achieved by mixing and matching coloured ribbons. They can be plaited or twisted and grouped into colours to cascade down a wrapped present.

## YOU WILL NEED
*Assortment of ribbons*
*Scissors*
*Double-sided tape*
*Metallic pen*

**1** One of the most straightforward ways to use ribbon is to curl it. This effect is achieved by pulling the ribbon through closed scissors to make it twist and fall into natural ringlets. Try doing this to different lengths and colours of ribbons and then attach them to your present.

**2** Another effective way to use ribbon is to plait it, using at least three different colours. Tape the ribbon ends together and plait to the required length. Secure and cut the ribbon ends.

**3** In this example a whole medley of ribbons in different colours and widths is plaited together in order to create a riot of colour. Tape and cut the ribbon ends.

**4** To give ribbon an individual look, decorate it by drawing a design taken from the wrapping paper with a metallic pen.

*Ribboncrafts*

# RIBBON WATCHSTRAP

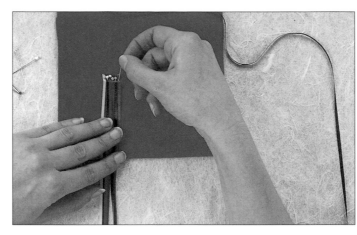

Knot a pretty watchstrap in someone's favourite colours to add a fashionable touch to an everyday timepiece.

## YOU WILL NEED
*Masking tape*
*Piece of felt*
*Pins*
*Approximately 1.5 m (1½ yd) lengths
    of 3 mm (⅛ in) ribbon in 5 colours*
*Watch face*
*Short length of wide silk ribbon*
*Needle and thread*
*Small buckle*
*Iron*

**1** Tape the piece of felt to a firm flat surface. Pin the ribbons at one end in a neat row onto the felt. Keep the ribbons flat and pin again 2.5 cm (1 in) down from the first row of pins.

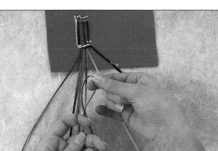

**2** Following the diagram, bring each ribbon over, under, and over the one next to it starting with the first ribbon on the left. Continue in this way and knot all the way to the right. The first ribbon on the left will then be the last ribbon on the right.

**3** Calculate the circumference of the watch-wearer's wrist. Continue knotting until you reach the halfway point on the strap. Thread the watch onto the ribbon, ensuring the ribbons lie flat across the back. Continue knotting until you reach the required length for the strap.

**4** Cover one end of the strap with a small piece of wide silk ribbon and sew it in place on one side. Thread on the buckle and sew down the wide ribbon. Cover the other end of the strap with a piece of wide ribbon and sew in place. Gently stretch the strap and press with a cool iron.

# NEEDLEWORK CRAFTS

## STITCHES

### Back stitch
Work back stitch from right to left, making small, even stitches forwards and backwards along the row, keeping the stitches of identical size.

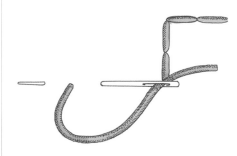

### Holbein stitch
This stitch is also known as double running stitch.

Work a row of evenly spaced stitches along the line to be stitched. Fill in the spaces left on the first row with stitches worked on the second row, this time going in the opposite direction.

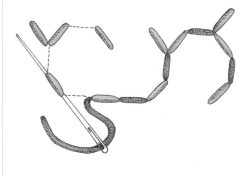

### Chain stitch
Work chain stitch downwards by making a series of loops of identical size. Remember to anchor the last loop in the row with a small straight stitch.

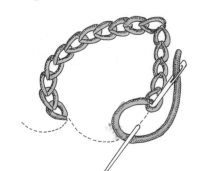

### Cross stitch
Begin by working a row of diagonal stitches from right to left, then complete the crosses with a second row of diagonal stitches worked in the opposite direction. Remember that the top diagonal stitches of each cross should always slant in the same direction, usually from bottom left to top right.

### Half cross stitch
If you work just the bottom diagonal stitches, the stitch is then called half cross stitch.

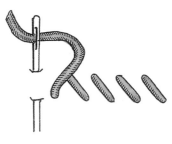

### Detached chain stitch
This stitch is also known as daisy stitch or lazy daisy stitch and it is actually a single chain stitch.

Work detached chain stitch in the same way as ordinary chain stitch, but anchor each loop with a small straight stitch before proceeding to make the next loop.

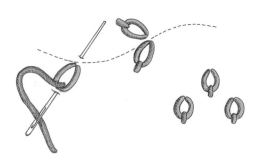

### Whipped back stitch
Work whipped back stitch in one or two colours of thread.

First, make a foundation row of ordinary back stitch, making the stitches slightly longer than usual. Using a second thread, whip over the back stitches from right to left, without picking up any fabric. Use a blunt-ended tapestry needle for the second thread to avoid splitting or snagging the stitches on the foundation row.

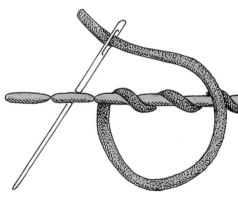

### French knot
Bring the thread through the fabric and hold it taut with your left hand. Twist the needle around the thread two or three times, then tighten the twists. Still holding the thread in your left hand, turn the needle and insert it into the fabric at the point where it originally emerged. Pull the needle and thread through the twists to complete the knot.

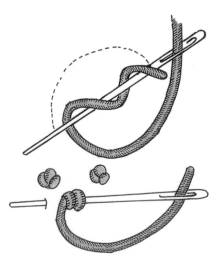

## Blanket stitch

Use blanket stitch as an edging stitch for appliqué as well as a surface stitch. You can vary the effect by making the upright stitches alternately long and short or graduate their lengths to form pyramid shapes.

Work blanket stitch from left to right, pulling the needle through the fabric over the top of the working thread. Space the stitches evenly along the row.

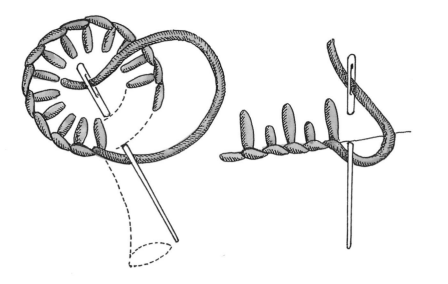

## TRANSFERRING A DESIGN

The two easiest ways of transferring a traced design onto a piece of fabric are by using dressmaker's carbon paper or a light source.

### Carbon paper

Place a piece of dressmaker's carbon paper with the ink side down on the right side of your fabric. Position the tracing on top, as shown, making sure the design is centred. Pin the layers together round the edge and place on a hard, flat surface. Draw round the outlines with a hard pencil, pressing firmly. Use blue or red carbon paper on light fabric and yellow carbon paper on dark fabric.

### Using a light source

This method works well with fine fabric such as cotton or silk. You can use a glass-topped table as shown, or alternatively rest a small sheet of glass or clear plastic between two dining chairs. On a bright, sunny day you can tape both tracing and fabric onto a window and transfer the design in the same way.

Place an adjustable lamp underneath the glass, directing the light upwards. Place the tracing on the glass and secure with masking tape. Position the fabric over the tracing, centring the design, and secure with more tape. Slowly trace the design with a soft, sharp pencil and take care to avoid dragging the fabric as you work.

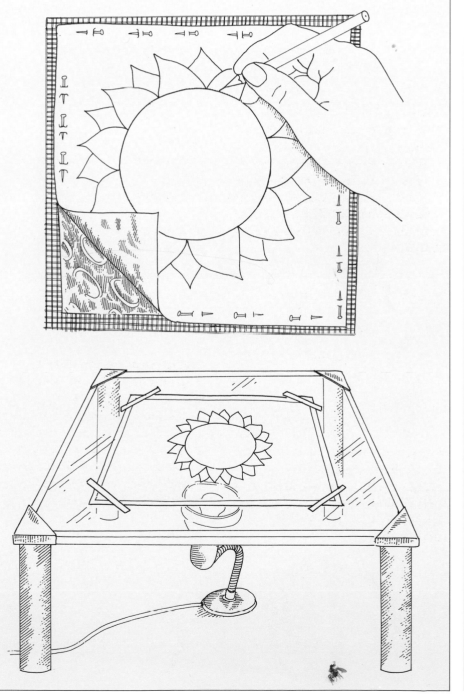

# ASSISI BOOKMARK

Assisi embroidery is originally from Italy and it is usually worked in two thread colours on a white or cream background. Here, the technique is used to work a design down the centre of a ready-made fabric bookmark.

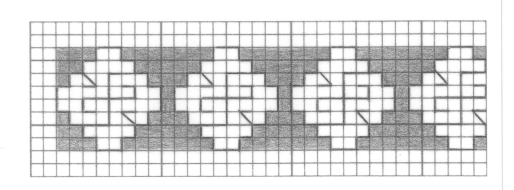

## YOU WILL NEED
*Ready-made white bookmark with 18-count fabric centre*
*Stranded cotton in terracotta and dark grey*
*Tapestry needle*

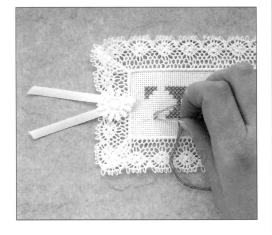

**1** Each coloured square on the chart represents one cross stitch worked over two woven blocks in the fabric. Following the chart, work the background areas in cross stitch using two strands of terracotta thread.

**2** Outline the cross stitch areas with Holbein stitch worked over two fabric blocks using two strands of dark grey thread, then work the linear details in the same way.

# STITCH SAMPLER GREETINGS CARD

This design gives you the opportunity to practise several embroidery stitches and try out new colour combinations. Arrange the rows of stitches in the form of a sampler and mount your embroidery in a ready-made card.

## YOU WILL NEED
*Ready-made cream greetings card with an oval aperture*
*Small piece of 18-count ainring in lemon yellow*
*Water-soluble embroidery marker*
*Scraps of stranded cotton in yellow, orange, tan, dark red and green or any other colour combination*
*Tapestry needle*
*Scissors*
*Steam iron*

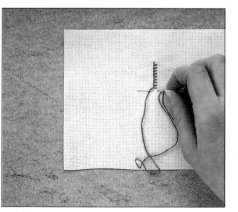

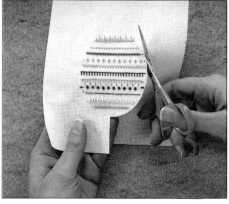

**1** Centre the greetings card aperture over the fabric and draw round the oval with the embroidery marker.

**2** Fill the oval with horizontal rows of blanket stitch, chain stitch, backstitch, half cross stitch and French knots, making sure you take the ends of each row beyond the oval outline. Use three strands of thread except for the French knots which are worked in six strands.

**3** Cut out 6 mm (¼ in) outside the oval outline. Immerse in cold water to remove marker and allow to dry. Press the embroidery on the wrong side with a cool iron and mount in the card following the manufacturer's instructions.

# BLACKWORK PAPERWEIGHT

Explore the delicate effect of blackwork, an embroidery technique used throughout Europe since the sixteenth century, by working this design and mounting it in a clear glass paperweight.

## YOU WILL NEED
*Small piece of 11-count pearl aida fabric in cream*
*Flower thread in black*
*Tapestry needle*
*Square glass craft paperweight*
*Sharp HB pencil*
*Scissors*

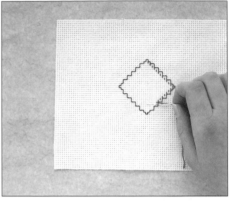

**1** Each square on the chart represents one woven block in the fabric. Embroider in Holbein stitch.

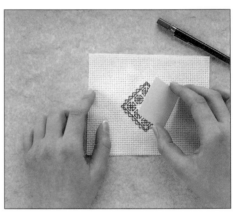

**2** Remove the card insert from the paperweight and centre it over the embroidery. Draw round the edge of the card with a sharp HB pencil and cut out along the line.

**3** Mount the embroidery in the paperweight following the manufacturer's instructions. Finish off the paperweight by pressing the self-adhesive backing in position.

# HOLLY GIFT TAG

This holly design is quick to embroider in half cross stitch, adding a bead every time you make a stitch.

## YOU WILL NEED
*Scraps of 18-count ainring in white*
*Stranded cotton in red and two*
    *shades of green*
*Small beads to match each of the*
    *thread colours*
*Tapestry needle*
*Ready-made cream gift tags*
*Scissors*
*Narrow sticky tape*
*Fine gold cord*

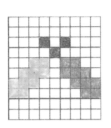

**1** Each coloured square on the chart represents one half cross stitch worked over two woven blocks in the fabric. Following the chart, work the design using two strands of thread, adding one bead in the appropriate colour with every stitch you make.

**2** Centre the holly motif in the gift tag aperture, cut away the surplus fabric and secure with strips of narrow sticky tape.

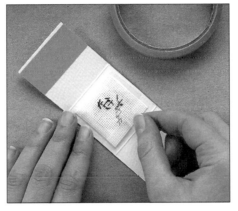

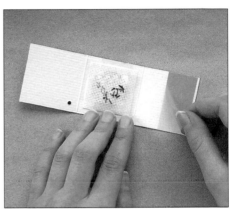

**3** Remove the backing strip from the gift tag flap, fold over card and press together with your fingers. Add a loop of fine gold cord and tie the tag on your parcel.

# INITIAL KEY RING

Organize your household keys by making each member of the family their own embroidered key ring bearing the appropriate initial.

## YOU WILL NEED
*Transparent plastic key ring complete with ring*
*Small piece of bright yellow cotton fabric*
*Sharp HB pencil*
*Tracing paper*
*Stranded cotton in blue*
*Crewel needle*
*Steam iron*
*Medium-weight iron-on interfacing*
*Scissors*

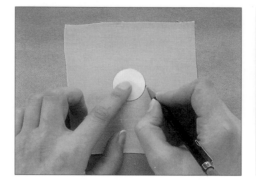

**1** Remove the card circle from the key fob and place it on the right side of the fabric. Draw round the card with a sharp HB pencil.

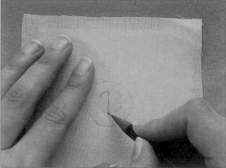

**2** Scale up and trace the initial and transfer it to the centre of the card circle using the pencil.

ABCDEFGHI
JKLMNOPQRS
TUVWXYZ

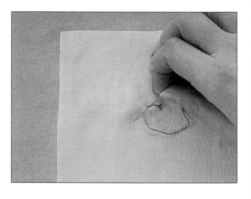

**3** Using two strands of blue thread in the crewel needle, embroider the outline of the initial in backstitch, then dot French knots at random over the solid areas.

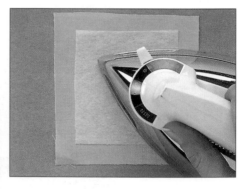

**4** Turn the embroidery over and iron a piece of medium-weight iron-on interfacing over the back. Cut out round the drawn circle and mount in the key ring following the manufacturer's instructions.

# FLORAL PICTURE

This delightful flower picture is embroidered in detached chain stitch and French knots using an assortment of soft, subtle shades of pink, mauve and green wool.

## YOU WILL NEED
*Circular brass frame with convex glass*
*Small piece of white fabric with a fairly open weave*
*Water-soluble embroidery marker*
*Steam iron*
*Medium-weight iron-on interfacing*
*Zephyr or Persian wool in three shades of pink, two shades of green, mauve and orange*
*Tapestry needle*

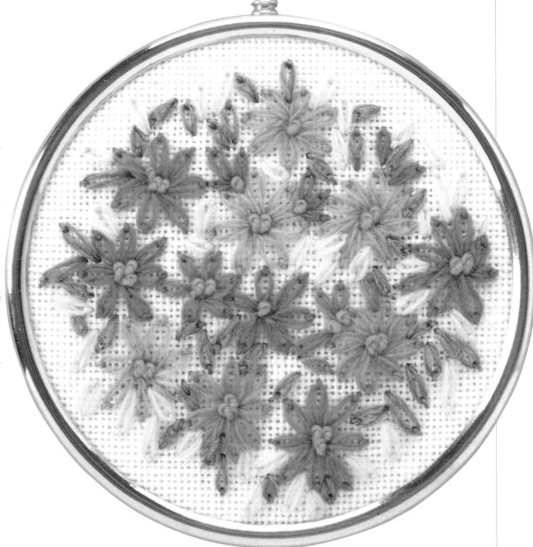

**1** Place the glass from the frame on the right side of the fabric. Draw round the glass with the marker. Turn the fabric over and iron a piece of medium-weight iron-on interfacing on top.

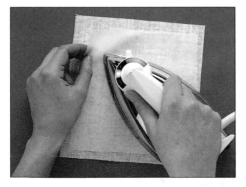

**2** On the right side, mark dots at random inside the circle. Each dot indicates the centre of a flower.

**3** Arranging the stitches in a circle round each dot, embroider the flowers in detached chain stitch, using two strands of the pink and mauve wools. Embroider the leaves in detached chain stitch, using two strands of green wool and dotting the stitches at random between the flowers. Finally, fill the centre of each flower with French knots using four strands of orange wool. Mount the embroidery in the frame following the manufacturer's instructions.

# FELT NEEDLECASE

Make this attractive needlecase from brightly coloured scraps of felt to keep your sewing and embroidery needles safe.

## YOU WILL NEED

*Stiff white card*
*Ruler*
*Scissors*
*Small pieces of fuchsia, pink, orange, green and yellow felt*
*Black felt-tip pen*
*Coin*
*Stranded cotton in yellow, orange and green*
*Crewel needle*
*Tacking (basting) thread in a contrasting colour*
*Sewing needle*

**1** Cut out a 9 cm × 14 cm (3½ in × 5½ in) rectangle from white card to make a template. Lay the template on the fuchsia felt, draw round it with the black felt-tip pen and cut out. Repeat with the pink and orange felt.

**2** Using a coin as a template, cut out a circle of both the green and yellow felt. Also cut out a small strip and a square of the fuchsia felt.

Arrange the shapes on half of the pink felt rectangle and attach them using blanket stitch and three strands of cotton with the crewel needle.

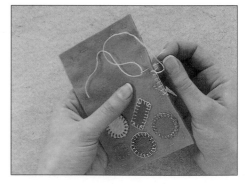

**3** Tack (baste) the pink and fuchsia felt rectangles together. Work a row of blanket stitch round the edge using three strands of yellow thread. With the fuchsia side facing, stitch the orange felt down the centre, then fold in half to make a book shape. You may need to trim the orange felt slightly round the edges with sharp scissors.

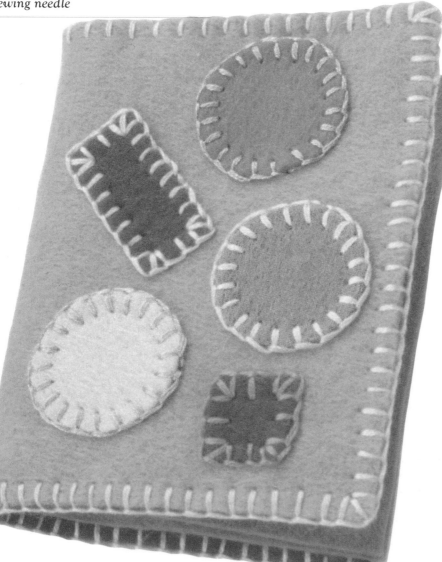

# HEART-SHAPED BOX

A porcelain box with an embroidered design set in the lid makes a lovely gift for a special friend. Fill the box with pot-pourri or some favourite bath pearls.

## YOU WILL NEED
*Tracing paper*
*Sharp HB pencil*
*Small piece of pink cotton or linen fabric*
*Stranded cotton in yellow, pink, light green and jade green*
*Crewel needle*
*Tapestry needle*
*Steam iron*
*Scissors*
*Heart-shaped porcelain craft box in pink*

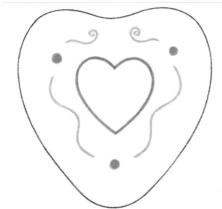

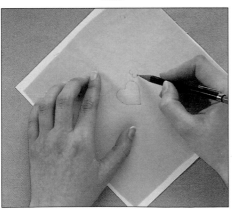

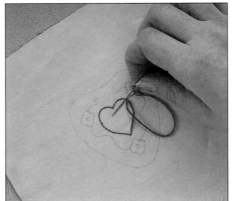

**1** Scale up the template to the desired size and transfer it to the right side of the fabric using a sharp HB pencil. Make sure you transfer each part of the design, including the heart-shaped cutting line.

**2** Following the colours shown on the template, embroider the design in whipped backstitch, chain stitch and French knots, using two strands of thread in the crewel needle. When working the whipping stage of the backstitch, use six strands of thread in the tapestry needle.

**3** Press the embroidery lightly on the wrong side with a cool iron. Cut out along the heart-shaped cutting line with a pair of sharp scissors. Mount the embroidery in the box lid following the manufacturer's instructions.

# BOW HANDKERCHIEF

Embroider this charming bow motif in one corner of a ready-made white handkerchief, perhaps matching the colour of the embroidery to a special outfit.

## YOU WILL NEED
*Tracing paper*
*White ready-made cotton or linen*
 *handkerchief*
*Water-soluble embroidery marker*
*Stranded cotton in turquoise*
*Crewel needle*
*Steam iron*

**1** Scale up and trace the bow motif from the template and transfer it to one corner of the handkerchief using the embroidery marker.

**2** Embroider the motif in chain stitch using two strands of thread. When the bow is complete, immerse the handkerchief in cold water to remove the embroidery marker outlines and allow to dry. Press on the wrong side with a cool iron.

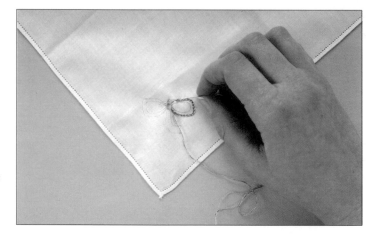

# CHERRY PLACE CARD

Place cards can add a really individual touch to a table setting, whether formal or informal. After the cards have been completed, use a gold felt-tip pen and your best handwriting to add the names.

## YOU WILL NEED
*Ready-made red place cards with aperture*
*Scraps of white silk or cotton fabric*
*Sharp HB pencil*
*Stranded cotton in red and green*
*Crewel needle*
*Scissors*
*Sticky tape*

**1** Lay the aperture on the place card over the right side of the fabric. Using a sharp HB pencil, mark a dot on the fabric to indicate the centre of each cherry.

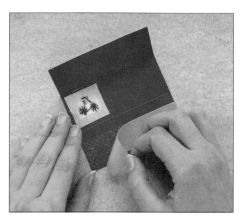

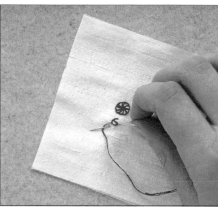

**2** Embroider blanket stitch in a circle round each dot using two strands of red thread. Work two lines of backstitch to join the cherries and make the stalks using two strands of green thread.

**3** Centre the cherry motif in the place card aperture, cut away the surplus fabric and secure with strips of narrow sticky tape. Remove the backing strip from the place card flap, fold over and press in position.

## STITCHES

### Jacquard stitch

Work a row of evenly sized diagonal stitches covering three vertical and three horizontal canvas threads. Arrange the stitches in steps of six, as shown. Next, work a row of tent stitches, following the stepped outline. Work alternate rows of the two stitches to fill the shape.

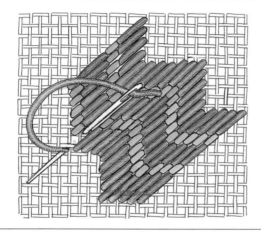

### Half cross stitch

Although this stitch looks the same as tent stitch on the right side, the working method for the two stitches is different. These two stitches should not be used on the same piece of needlepoint as they 'pull' and distort the canvas in different directions.

Work rows of small diagonal stitches from top to bottom of the shape, as shown.

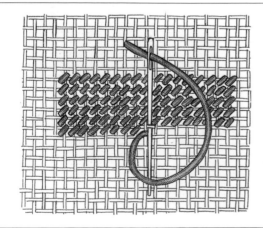

### Slanting satin stitch

This versatile stitch can be worked in rows or alternatively stepped to form a zigzag line. It can also be used to embroider small blocks by graduating the lengths of the stitches to fill the corners.

Work diagonal stitches spanning the same number of vertical and horizontal canvas threads, usually two, three or four.

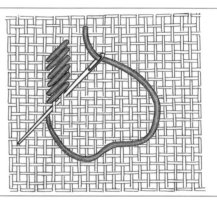

### Brighton stitch

Work blocks of five diagonal stitches of graduated length. Arrange the blocks in rows, changing the direction of the slant in alternate rows. Each new row of blocks should be the mirror image of the row above.

After the blocks have been completed, work two straight stitches in a contrasting colour to form an upright cross in the gap between each block.

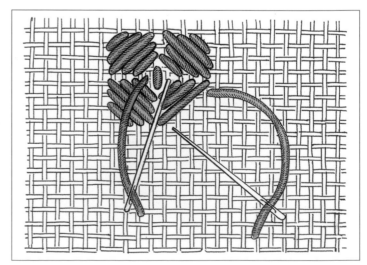

## Mosaic stitch

Each mosaic stitch block consists of one diagonal stitch worked over two vertical and two horizontal canvas threads at the centre of two short diagonal stitches. Stitch the blocks individually when embroidering a multicoloured design.

To work background areas in mosaic stitch, work each horizontal row over two journeys. Begin at the top left-hand side and work the first short stitch and the long stitch of each block. On the second journey, complete each block by filling in the remaining short stitch.

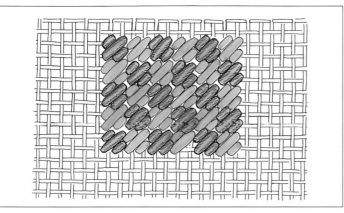

## Florentine stitch

Work vertical straight stitches over the required number of horizontal canvas threads, usually four or six, and arrange them in a step sequence to form zigzag rows. Work subsequent rows of stitches in different colours to fill the canvas above and below the first row, following the contours carefully.

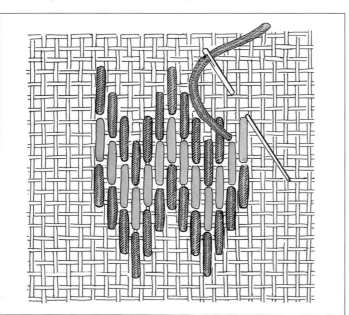

## Tent stitch

There are two methods of working tent stitch:

Use the diagonal method shown in the top stitches for working large areas as this method is less likely to pull the canvas out of shape. Work up and down in diagonal rows, making small diagonal stitches over one intersection of the canvas.

Use the second method for embroidering details and single lines. Begin at the lower edge of the shape and work in horizontal rows as shown in the bottom stitches.

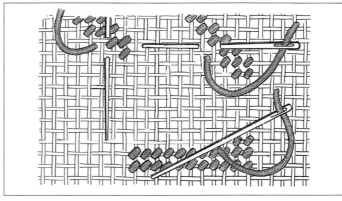

## Double Leviathan stitch

Begin by working a large cross over a square of four canvas threads. Work a series of crossing stitches over the top, following the sequence shown in the diagram. Take care to follow the diagrams carefully to achieve the correct result.

# BOOKMARK

This bookmark is simple to embroider in Jacquard stitch using nine shades of green thread. You may prefer to use a different colour combination, perhaps one which allows you to use up any oddments of stranded cotton you have.

## YOU WILL NEED
*Ruler*
*Small piece of 17-mesh needlepoint*
  *canvas*
*Waterproof black fine felt-tip pen*
*Stranded cotton in nine shades of*
  *green*
*Tapestry needle*
*Scissors*
*Ready-made bookmark with aperture*
*Sticky tape*

**1** Mark out a rectangle, slightly larger than the bookmark aperture, on the canvas using a black felt-tip pen.

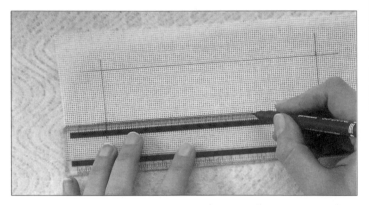

**2** Following the chart, cover the rectangle with rows of Jacquard stitch using six strands of cotton. Use eight colours in rotation to stitch the wide rows and the ninth colour to stitch all the narrow rows.

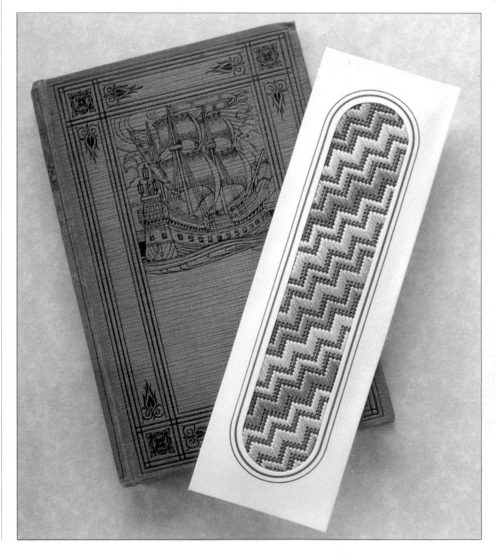

**3** Cut out the embroidery leaving a border of 6 mm (¼ in) of unworked canvas all round. Centre the embroidery in the bookmark aperture and secure with narrow sticky tape. Fold over the bookmark and press together with your fingers.

# BUTTERFLY
# PINCUSHION

Make a needlepoint pincushion decorated with a delicate butterfly motif to keep your pins safe. Make another to give to a friend, choosing a different colour combination.

## YOU WILL NEED
*Small piece of 17-mesh needlepoint canvas*
*Stranded cotton in the following colours: 1 skein each of purple, pale blue, kingfisher blue, turquoise and green; 2 skeins of yellow*
*Tapestry needle*
*Scissors*
*Needle and tacking (basting) thread*
*Small piece of felt to match one of the thread colours*
*Crewel needle*
*Polyester stuffing (batting)*
*Knitting needle*
*Pinking shears*

**1** Each coloured square on the chart represents one mosaic stitch. Work the butterfly motif in mosaic stitch using six strands of thread in the tapestry needle.

**2** Cut away the surplus canvas round the embroidery leaving a border of 12 mm (½ in). Turn under and tack (baste). Cut out a piece of felt 12 mm (½ in) larger all round than the embroidery. Centre the embroidery on the felt and stitch together with running stitches, using three strands of matching cotton in the crewel needle and leaving a small gap along one side for stuffing the pincushion.

**3** Stuff the pincushion using a knitting needle to manoeuvre the stuffing (batting) right into the corners. Sew up the gap, then cut round the felt with pinking shears.

# PRETTY NAPKIN RING

Decorate a plain silver- or gold-coloured napkin ring with a strip of perforated paper embroidered with a simple geometric design in half cross stitch.

## YOU WILL NEED
*Small piece of white perforated paper*
*Scissors*
*Plain silver- or gold-coloured napkin ring*
*Stranded cotton in yellow, blue and turquoise*
*Tapestry needle*
*Fabric glue*
*Small paintbrush*
*Contact adhesive*

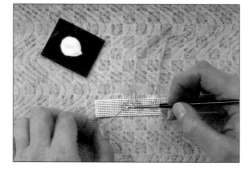

**1** Cut out a strip of perforated paper large enough to fit round the napkin ring.

**2** Each coloured square on the chart represents one half cross stitch. Following the chart, work the design along the paper strip using two strands of thread and leaving both ends of the thread free.

**3** Secure the loose threads on the wrong side with a small dab of fabric glue on a paintbrush. Allow to dry, then snip off the thread ends.

**4** Using contact adhesive, stick the embroidered strip in place round the napkin ring.

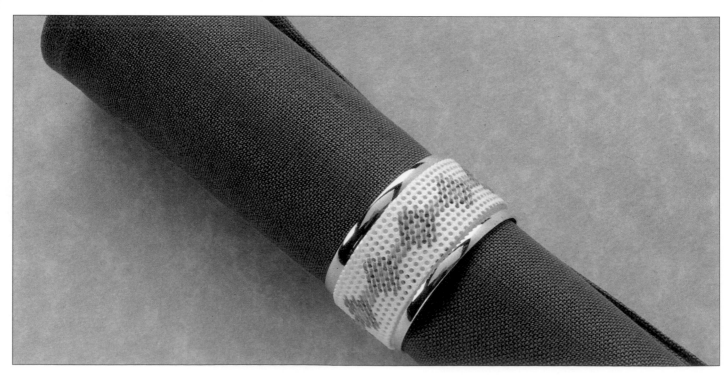

# FLORENTINE EVENING BAG

Make this tiny evening bag to hold keys, handkerchief and lipstick on a special night out, co-ordinating the colour scheme with a favourite outfit.

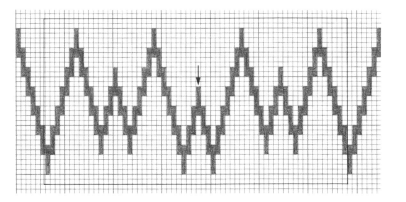

## YOU WILL NEED
*Ruler*
*Small piece of 22-mesh needlepoint canvas*
*Waterproof black fine felt-tip pen*
*Stranded cotton in the following colours: 2 skeins of purple; 1 skein each of pale blue, blue and kingfisher blue; plus 1 skein to match your fabric colour*
*Tapestry needle*
*Metallic-effect silver yarn*
*Scissors*
*Sewing needle*
*Tacking (basting) thread in a contrasting colour*
*Remnant of heavy silk to match one of the thread colours*
*Crewel needle*
*Braid for shoulder strap*

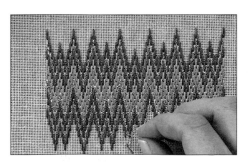

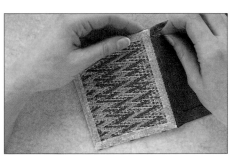

**1** Mark out a rectangle 10 cm × 12 cm (4 in × 4¾ in) on the canvas using a black felt-tip pen. Following the chart and beginning at the centre, work one row of Florentine stitch using six strands of the purple thread in the tapestry needle. Work the remaining rows following the zigzag design on the chart. Use six strands of thread throughout, except for the silver yarn which is used singly.

**2** Cut out the embroidery leaving a border of 12 mm (½ in) all round. Turn under the raw edges and tack (baste). Cut out a piece of silk 14 × 25 cm (5½ × 10 in), turn under 12 mm (½ in) round the edge and tack (baste). With right sides together, place the embroidery over the silk, matching the edges as shown, and stitch together using two strands of matching thread in the crewel needle.

**3** Cut out a second piece of silk 12 mm (½ in) larger all round than the joined piece of embroidery and silk. Turn under 12 mm (½ in) all round and tack (baste). Place wrong sides together and stitch round the edges using two strands of thread as before. Turn up about one-third of the silk to form a flap and stitch along the sides. Stitch the braid under the flap to make a strap.

# SUNGLASSES CASE

This sturdy case for sunglasses is embroidered in Brighton stitch using brightly coloured tapestry wool, then lined and backed with silk.

## YOU WILL NEED
*Ruler*
*Waterproof black fine felt-tip pen*
*Small piece of 11-mesh single-thread canvas*
*Tapestry wool in the following colours: 1 skein of yellow; 3 skeins of green*
*Tapestry needle*
*Scissors*
*Sewing needle*
*Tacking (basting) thread in a contrasting colour*
*Small piece of green silk*
*Stranded cotton to match the silk fabric*
*Crewel needle*

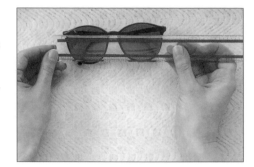

**1** Measure the sunglasses to calculate how large the case needs to be. Mark out a rectangle to this size on the canvas using a black pen. To work Brighton stitch correctly, the area must divide equally into blocks of four threads.

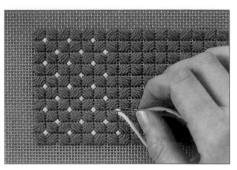

**2** Cover the rectangle with Brighton stitch using green wool for the straight stitches and yellow wool for the crosses.

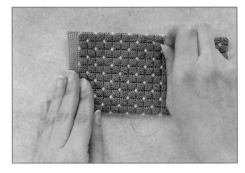

**3** Cut out the embroidery leaving a border of 12 mm (½ in) all round. Turn under the raw edges and tack (baste). Cut out three pieces of green silk 12 mm (½ in) larger all round than the embroidery. Turn under 12 mm (½ in) round the edge of each piece and tack (baste).

**4** Place the embroidery and one piece of fabric with wrong sides together. Stitch round the edge using two strands of matching cotton in a crewel needle. To make the back, place the remaining two pieces of green silk with wrong sides together and stitch round the edge. Place the back and front with wrong sides together and stitch round three sides.

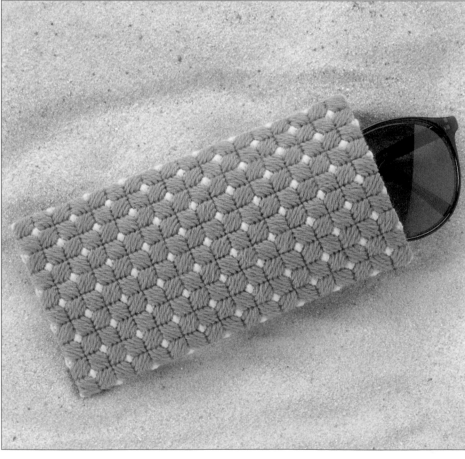

# MEMENTO BOX

Make this attractive box to keep your tiny bits and pieces – for example, foreign coins, paper clips or rubber bands – and prevent them from getting lost.

## YOU WILL NEED
*Turned wooden craft box with lid*
*Waterproof black fine felt-tip pen*
*Small piece of 17-mesh needlepoint canvas*
*Stranded cotton in orange, light green, mid green and rust*
*Tapestry needle*
*Scissors*

**1** Remove the card circle from the lid. Place it on the canvas and draw round it with a black felt-tip pen.

**2** Each square on the chart represents one canvas intersection. Work the design in slanting satin stitch, using six strands of thread.

**3** Cut out the embroidery slightly inside the marked line. Mount in the box lid following the manufacturer's instructions.

# HAIR CLIP

Transform a plain brown hair clip into a party piece by adding a strip of gold perforated paper embroidered with flower motifs.

## YOU WILL NEED
*Scissors*
*Small piece of gold perforated paper*
*Hair clip*
*Stranded cotton in green and pink*
*Tapestry needle*
*Fabric glue*
*Small paintbrush*
*Double-sided sticky tape*

**1** Cut out a strip of perforated paper large enough to cover the hair clip. Each coloured square on the chart represents one tent stitch.

**2** Following the chart, work a motif at each end of the strip in tent stitch using three strands of thread.

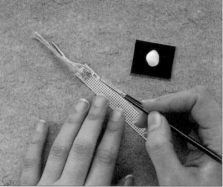

**3** Secure the loose threads on the wrong side with a small dab of fabric adhesive on a paintbrush. Allow to dry thoroughly, then snip off the thread ends. Cover the back of the perforated paper with double-sided sticky tape, trimming away the surplus and taking care not to snip into the paper. Peel off the backing paper and press in position on the hair clip.

# PHOTOGRAPH FRAME

Frame a favourite photograph with this needlepoint frame. The embroidery is strengthened with fabric adhesive so the surplus canvas can be cut away to leave a shaped edge.

## YOU WILL NEED
*Small piece of 17-mesh needlepoint canvas*
*Stranded cotton in beige, brown and rust*
*Tapestry needle*
*Scissors*
*Fabric adhesive*
*Craft knife*
*Cream card for mount to fit frame*
*Masking tape*
*12.5 cm × 18 cm (5 in × 7 in) picture frame*

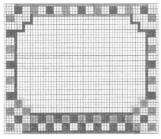

**1** Work the design from the chart in tent stitch and blocks of slanting satin stitch using six strands of thread.

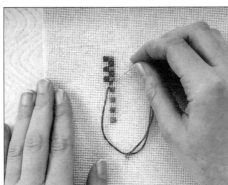

**2** Using a small, sharp pair of scissors, cut away the surplus canvas carefully, close to the inner row of stitching. Seal and strengthen the wrong side of the stitches by spreading a thin layer of fabric adhesive over them.

**3** Using a craft knife, cut out a rectangular window in the cream card to accommodate the embroidery in the centre. Secure the embroidery in position with strips of masking tape.

**4** Centre the photograph in the aperture and secure it in position, face down, with strips of masking tape. Insert in the picture frame.

# TULIP BOX

This silver-plated box is decorated with an embroidered lid featuring an all-over design of tulips stitched in fine wool thread.

## YOU WILL NEED
*Silver-plated craft box*
*Small piece of 17-mesh needlepoint*
*  canvas*
*Waterproof black fine felt-tip pen*
*Crewel wool in the following colours: 1*
*  skein each of blue, yellow, pink,*
*  and green; 2 skeins of cream*
*Tapestry needle*
*Scissors*

**1** Remove the card circle from the lid. Place it on the canvas and draw round it with a black felt-tip pen.

**2** Each coloured square on the chart represents one tent stitch. Embroider the design in tent stitch using double thread. Begin by embroidering the blue lines, then the flowers and finally fill in the background.

**3** Cut out the embroidery slightly inside the marked line. Mount in the box lid following the manufacturer's instructions.

# CHRISTMAS CARD

Send your Christmas greetings with this unusual embroidered card featuring a three-dimensional tree set against a coloured background.

## YOU WILL NEED

*Small piece of 22-mesh needlepoint canvas*
*Stranded cotton, red, two shades of green and brown*
*Metallic-effect gold yarn*
*Tapestry needle*
*Green felt-tip pen*
*Ready-made greetings card with an oval aperture*
*Scissors*
*Sticky tape*

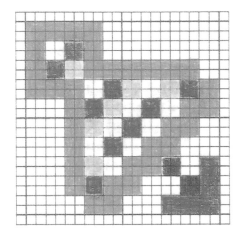

**1** Each coloured square on the chart represents one double leviathan stitch. Work the tree design in double leviathan stitch using six strands of stranded cotton and one strand of gold yarn.

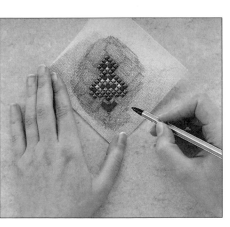

**2** Colour in the canvas background carefully with the green pen. Allow to dry thoroughly.

**3** Centre the design in the card aperture and cut away the surplus canvas. Mount in the card with sticky tape following the manufacturer's instructions.

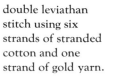

# CROSS STITCH TECHNIQUES

## STITCHES

### Cross stitch

There is more than one method of working cross stitch, but you should remember that the top diagonal stitches of each cross should always slant in the same direction, usually from bottom left to top right.

Use the first method for working individual stitches and small details on the designs, making sure you complete each cross before proceeding to the next one.

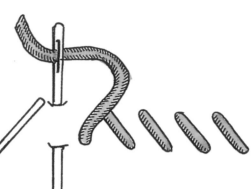

Use the second method for embroidering cross stitch over large areas as it will help you to achieve a more evenly stitched result. Begin by working a row of diagonal stitches from right to left, then complete the crosses with a second row of diagonal stitches worked in the opposite direction.

### Half cross stitch

If you work just the bottom diagonal stitches, using either of the two methods shown, the stitch is then called half cross stitch.

### Back stitch

Work back stitch from right to left, making small, even stitches forwards and backwards along the row, keeping the stitches of identical size.

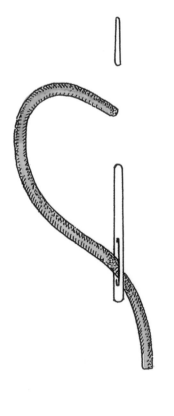

## USING STRANDED COTTON

Most of the projects in this chapter are embroidered with stranded cotton. This consists of six separate strands of thread loosely twisted together. When a project requires two or three strands, first cut a length about 38 cm (15 in) long from the skein, then separate all six strands and combine them once again to give the required thickness.

## CROSS STITCH CANVAS

Cross stitch fabrics come in various mesh sizes, or 'counts'. If the size specified in a pattern is not available, use the next size up or down. The design will appear slightly enlarged or condensed but the pattern will not be distorted.

## CRAFT BOXES

Special craft boxes are readily available from handicrafts suppliers and haberdashery departments in large stores. These boxes come in a range of sizes and shapes and are an excellent way of displaying a special needlework design, as well as being a delightful gift. The types available include wood, brass and silver.

## STARTING AND FINISHING

Do not begin with a knot at the end of your thread as this can cause an unsightly lump when your project is finished, or it may work loose and cause the stitching to unravel. Instead, secure your thread by making one or two stitches in a space which will be covered by the embroidery. When the length of thread is nearly used up, slide the needle under a group of stitches on the wrong side for about 1 cm (½ in) to anchor the thread, then cut off the loose end. You can also use this method to secure a new thread in a group of existing stitches.

## USING AN EMBROIDERY HOOP

An embroidery hoop will help you to stitch more evenly and cause minimum distortion to the fabric. A hoop consists of two rings placed one inside the other with the fabric sandwiched tightly in between. The rings are secured by a screw on the outer ring.

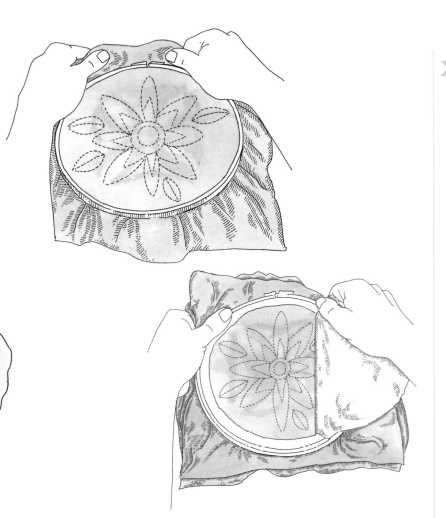

1 Spread the fabric, right side up, over the smaller hoop and press the larger hoop over the top. Tighten the screw lightly, then gently pull the fabric with your fingers until it is evenly stretched. Tighten the screw fully to hold the fabric in place.

2 On large projects, you will need to move the hoop along after one portion of the design has been completed. Protect the embroidery already worked from marks by spreading white tissue paper over the right side of the fabric before it is remounted in the hoop. Tear away the paper to expose the next area to be stitched.

## WORKING FROM A CHART

Read the instructions for each design carefully before you begin to stitch. They will tell you how to mark the position of the embroidery on the fabric, and at which point on the chart you should begin stitching from. You will need to mark your starting point on the chart with a soft pencil so that the mark can be erased later.

Begin stitching from the correct point and work outwards, remembering that each coloured square on the chart represents one cross stitch to be embroidered on the fabric. The instructions will also tell you the number of woven fabric blocks you need to cover with each stitch so that the design will work out to the correct size.

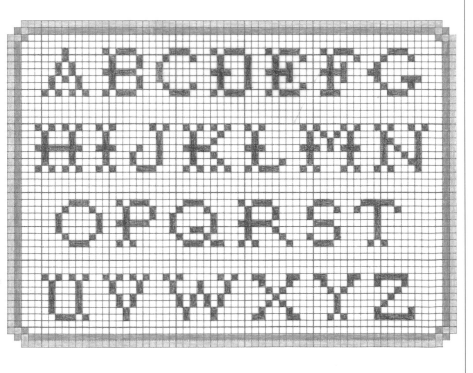

# DECORATIVE TABLE MATS

A set of decorated table mats looks attractive on a polished dining table and help to protect the surface. Make matching napkins for a co-ordinated table setting.

## YOU WILL NEED

For each mat: 42 cm × 30 cm (16½ in × 12 in) of 18-count ainring in ivory
Sewing needle
Tacking (basting) thread in a contrasting colour
Stranded cotton in pink, bright green and dark green (two skeins of the pink thread and two skeins of each of the green threads will be sufficient to embroider six table mats)
Tapestry needle
Pins
Sewing thread to match the fabric

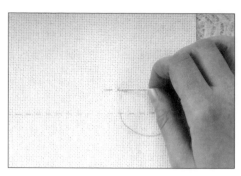

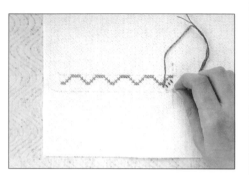

**1** Mark the position of the embroidered strip about 7.5 cm (3 in) from one end of the fabric with two rows of tacking spaced 14 fabric blocks apart. Also mark the centre of the strip with a row of tacking (basting).

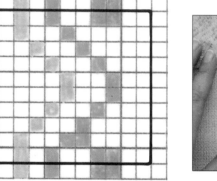

**2** Each coloured square on the chart represents one cross stitch worked over two woven blocks in the fabric. Following the chart, embroider the design in cross stitch using three strands of thread and working outwards from the centre of the strip.

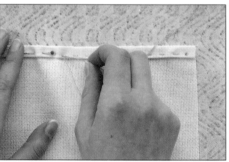

**3** Taking care to fold over the corners neatly, turn a narrow double hem round the edge of the table mat, pinning and tacking (basting) in place. Secure with a row of hand or machine stitches using matching thread.

# GEOMETRIC BUTTONS

This set of cross stitch buttons will liven up a plain knitted jacket or coat. To create a different effect, substitute a dark fabric for the white used here and choose pastel threads.

## YOU WILL NEED
*Scissors*
*Thin card*
*Six button moulds*
*Scraps of 14-count fine aida in antique white*
*Pins*
*Sharp HB pencil*
*Stranded cotton in red, blue and green*
*Tapestry needle*

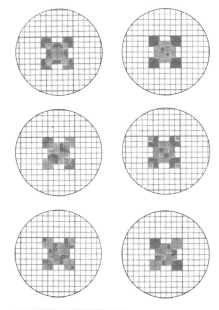

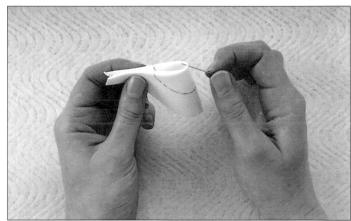

**1** Cut out the correct size of circle for the chosen button moulds in thin card and use this as a template. Lay the circle on the fabric and draw round it with a sharp HB pencil. Fold the fabric in four and mark the centre with a pin.

**2** Each coloured square on the chart represents one cross stitch worked over one woven block in the fabric. Following the chart, work the design in cross stitch using two strands of thread. Work out from the centre.

**3** Cut out the fabric around the pencil line and stretch over the button mould following the manufacturer's instructions.

**4** Attach the button backs, following the manufacturer's instructions and making sure the design will be upright on the front of each button when it is attached to the garment.

*Cross Stitch*

107

# WEDDING KEEPSAKE

This charming personalized wedding keepsake is sure to delight a newly-wed couple.

## YOU WILL NEED

*Small piece of 11-count pearl aida in antique white*
*Flower thread in two shades of pink, mid blue, navy blue and green*
*Sewing needle*
*Tacking (basting) thread in a contrasting colour*
*Tapestry needle*
*Oval silver-plated frame*
*Sharp HB pencil*
*Scissors*

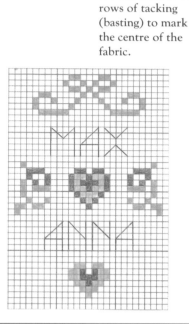

**1** Work vertical and horizontal rows of tacking (basting) to mark the centre of the fabric.

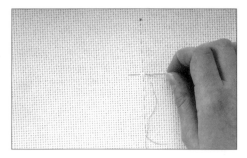

**2** Each coloured square on the chart represents one cross stitch worked over one woven block in the fabric. Embroider the lettering in back-stitch worked over one fabric block.

**3** Remove the acetate shape from the silver frame and lay it over the finished embroidery. Draw round the acetate with a sharp HB pencil.

**4** Cut out the embroidery slightly inside the pencil line. Mount in the frame following the manufacturer's instructions.

# ALPHABET
# SAMPLER

Many antique samplers feature a
variety of alphabets, both large and
small. You may like to add your
name below the lowest row of letters
on this sampler using a backstitch
alphabet.

## YOU WILL NEED
*Sewing needle*
*Tacking (basting) thread in a*
*  contrasting colour*
*Small piece of 11-count pearl aida in*
*  cream*
*Stranded cotton in dark pink,*
*  kingfisher blue and turquoise*
*Tapestry needle*
*Wooden cross frame*
*Scissors*
*Button thread for lacing*

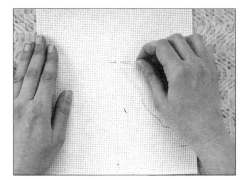

**1** Work vertical
and horizontal
rows of tacking
(basting) to mark
the centre of the
fabric.

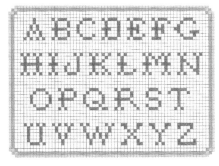

**2** Each coloured
square on the
chart represents one
cross stitch worked
over one woven
block in the fabric.
Following the chart,
embroider the
design in cross
stitch using three
strands of cotton.

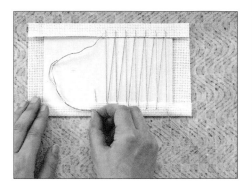

**3** Remove the
backing card
from the frame and
centre it over the
wrong side of the
finished embroid-
ery. Cut away the
surplus fabric
leaving a border of
5 cm (2 in) all
round. Fold over
the fabric at the top
and bottom of the
card and, using
button thread,
make long stitches
between the two
fabric edges. Knot
the thread at one
end, tighten the
stitches and secure
the other end of the
thread. Repeat
along the other two
sides. Mount in the
frame.

# DECORATIVE TOWEL

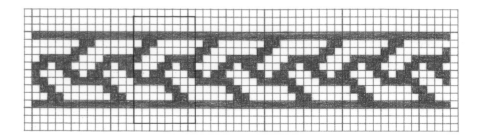

Transform a small plain white towel into a decorative feature by adding a band of embroidery along one end. You could make the band longer and decorate a bath towel to match.

## YOU WILL NEED

*7.5 cm (3 in) wide strip of 11-count pearl aida in white (the strip should be at least 5 cm (2 in) longer than the width of the towel)*
*Tacking (basting) thread in a contrasting colour*
*Sewing needle*
*Stranded cotton in blue*
*Tapestry needle*
*Scissors*
*Pins*
*Small white towel*
*Sewing thread to match the fabric*

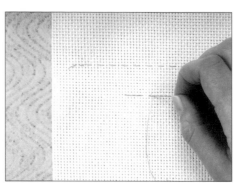

**1** Mark the position of the embroidery on the fabric strip by tacking (basting) two parallel lines 10 blocks apart.

**2** Each coloured square on the chart represents one cross stitch worked over one woven block in the fabric. Following the chart, embroider the design in cross stitch using two strands of thread.

**3** Turn in the raw edges round the embroidery, leaving two unworked fabric blocks along the long edges, and tack (baste). Cut away the surplus fabric on the wrong side. Pin the strip to the towel about 2.5 cm (1 in) from the edge and secure by working a row of backstitch round the edge using matching sewing thread. Work the stitches along the row of holes one block from the folded edge.

# CROSS-STITCH VALENTINE

This pretty Valentine can be framed and treasured as a keepsake.

## YOU WILL NEED
Pencil
Graph paper
Ruler
18-count ainring in cream
Embroidery threads
Embroidery needle and tacking
    (basting) thread
Soft cloth
Steam iron
Card
Strong clear glue
White card

**1** Scale up the design and transfer onto graph paper making one square equal to one cross-stitch. Measure the fabric and mark the centre with lines of tacking (basting) stitches.

**2** Using three strands of embroidery thread and starting from the top left, follow the chart.

**3** Cover the completed design with a damp cloth and press with an iron. Stretch the design over a piece of card and attach with zigzag stitches. Stick the design onto a piece of white card.

# EMBROIDERED NAPKINS

Use this cross stitch design to embroider a set of napkins to brighten up a dinner table. The same design could also be used to decorate table mats.

## YOU WILL NEED

*For each napkin: 33 cm (13 in) square*
*of 18-count ainring in ivory*
*Needle and tacking (basting) thread*
*in a contrasting colour*
*Stranded cotton in two shades of pink,*
*bright green and dark green (one*
*skein of each of the pink threads*
*and two skeins of each of the green*
*threads will be sufficient to*
*embroider six napkins)*
*Tapestry needle*
*Pins*
*Sewing thread to match the fabric*

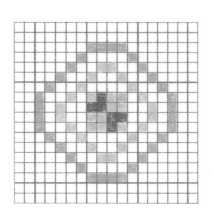

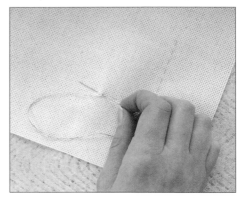

**1** Mark the position of the embroidered corner motif about 5 cm (2 in) from adjacent sides of the fabric with two rows of tacking (basting).

**2** Each coloured square on the chart represents one cross stitch worked over two woven blocks in the fabric.

Following the chart, embroider the design in cross stitch using three strands of thread.

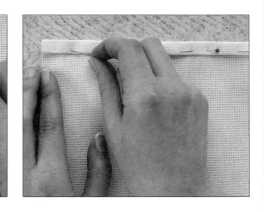

**3** Taking care to fold over the corners neatly, turn a narrow double hem round the edge of the napkin, pinning and tacking (basting) in place. Secure with a row of hand or machine stitches using matching thread.

# CRYSTAL BATHROOM JAR

A hand-cut lead crystal jar with a silver-plated lid featuring an embroidered pansy motif adds a touch of luxury to any bathroom.

## YOU WILL NEED
*Sewing needle*
*Tacking (basting) thread in a contrasting colour*
*Small piece of 11-count pearl aida in antique white*
*Stranded cotton in two shades of yellow, fuchsia pink, wine, two shades of mauve, lavender, purple and black*
*Tapestry needle*
*Crystal craft jar with silver-plated lid*
*Sharp HB pencil*
*Scissors*

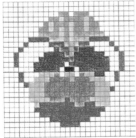

**1** Work vertical and horizontal rows of tacking to mark the centre of the fabric.

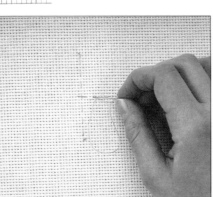

**2** Each coloured square on the chart represents one cross stitch worked over one woven block in the fabric. Following the chart, embroider the design in cross stitch using three strands of thread and working from the centre out.

**3** Remove the acetate shape from the jar lid and lay it over the finished embroidery. Draw round the acetate with a sharp HB pencil.

**4** Cut out the embroidery slightly inside the pencil line. Mount in the jar lid following the manufacturer's instructions.

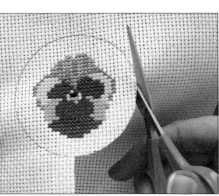

# SILVER PENDANT

A silver-plated pendant is the perfect way to display a tiny piece of beautifully stitched embroidery with a small-scale design.

## YOU WILL NEED

*Oval silver-plated craft pendant and chain*
*Small piece of 18-count ainring in white*
*Sharp HB pencil*
*Stranded cotton in yellow, orange, light green and dark green*
*Crewel needle*
*Scissors*

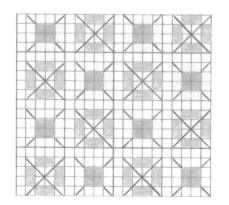

**1** Remove the card shape from the pendant and lay it on the fabric. Draw round the card with a pencil.

**2** Each coloured square on the chart represents one cross stitch worked over one woven block in the fabric. Following the chart, embroider the design in cross stitch using two strands of thread. Embroider the linear details in half cross stitch worked over one fabric block using two strands of dark green thread.

**3** Cut out the embroidery slightly inside the pencil line. Mount in the pendant following the manufacturer's instructions.

# CHRISTMAS TREE DECORATIONS

Hand-embroidered Christmas decorations in shaped golden frames will make your tree trimming a talking point year after year.

## YOU WILL NEED

*Small pieces of 11-count pearl aida in white*

*Stranded cotton in red, dark red, light green, mid green, dark green and brown*

*Tapestry needle*

*Metallic-effect gold yarn*

*Small gold beads*

*Shaped gold-coloured craft Christmas frames with shaped red felt self-adhesive backing*

*Sharp HB pencil*

*Scissors*

*Narrow red ribbon for hanging*

 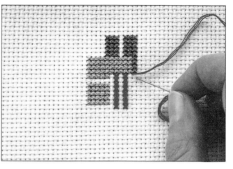

**1** Each coloured square on the chart represents one cross stitch worked over one woven block in the fabric. Work the designs in cross stitch using three strands of thread (or one strand of gold yarn).

**2** Outline the striped package in backstitch using two strands of brown thread. Add straight stitches and beads to the tree design.

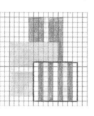 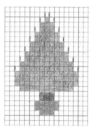

**3** Centre the frames over the embroidered motifs and draw round the outsides with a sharp HB pencil.

**4** Cut out the embroideries slightly inside the pencil lines. Mount in the frames following the manufacturer's instructions. To finish, add the red felt backing and red ribbon for hanging.

*Knitting abbreviations*
k = knit
p = purl
st(s) = stitch(es)
beg = beginning
inc = increase
tog = together
st st = stocking stitch
* * = instructions shown between
the asterisks must be repeated

## THE BASIC STITCHES

*Knit stitch*
With the yarn at the back of the work, insert the right-hand needle through the first stitch on the left-hand needle, wind the yarn over the right-hand needle, pull through a loop, then slip the original stitch off the left-hand needle. Repeat along the row until all the stitches have been transferred to the right-hand needle.

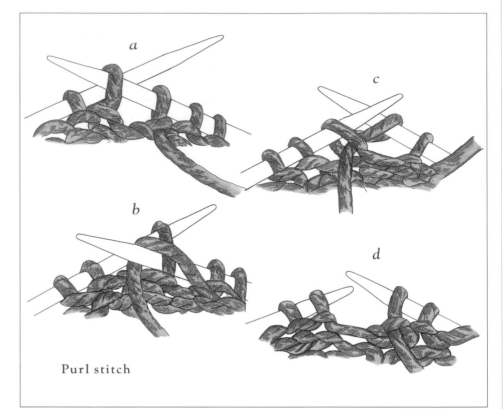

Purl stitch

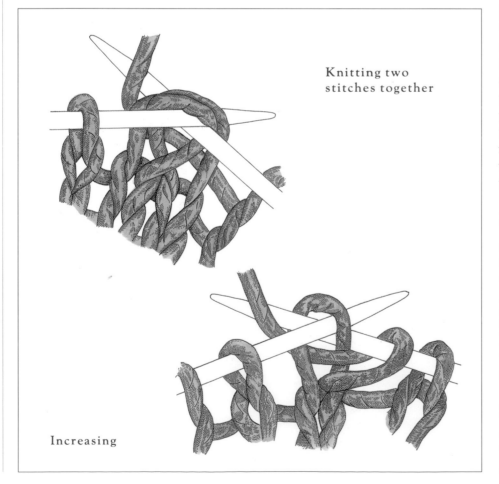

Knitting two stitches together

Increasing

*Purl stitch*
With the yarn at the front of the work, insert the right-hand needle through the front of the first stitch on the left-hand needle (a), wind the yarn round the left-hand needle (b), pull through a loop to the back (c), then slip the stitch off the left-hand needle (d). Repeat along the row until all the stitches have been transferred to the right-hand needle.

*Stocking and garter stitch*
To work stocking stitch, work alternate rows of knit and purl stitches. To work garter stitch, work every row knit.

*Knitting two stitches together*
Insert the right-hand needle through two stitches on the left-hand needle and knit them together.

*Increasing*
Knit or purl into the stitch in the usual way, then knit again into the back of the loop before slipping the stitch off the left-hand needle.

## Crochet abbreviations

ss = slip stitch
ch = chain stitch
dc = double crochet (= US single crochet)
tr = treble (= US double crochet)
dtr = double treble
rep = repeat
st(s) = stitch(es)
\* = stitches shown after this sign must be repeated from this point
( ) = the stitch combination enclosed in brackets must be repeated in the order shown

## THE BASIC STITCHES

### Chain stitch

Wrap the yarn over the hook (a) and draw the yarn through to make a new loop (b).

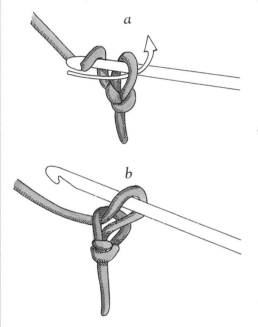

### Slip stitch

Insert the hook in the work, wrap the yarn over the hook, then draw the yarn through both the work and the loop on the hook in one movement.

### Double treble

Wrap the yarn over the hook twice and insert the hook in the work (a), wrap the yarn over the hook and draw the yarn through the work only (b) so there are now four loops on the hook, wrap the yarn again and draw the yarn through the first two loops on the hook (c), wrap the yarn and draw the yarn through the next two loops only (d), wrap the yarn and draw through the remaining two loops on the hook (e).

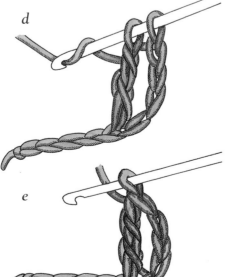

### Double crochet (US Treble crochet)

Insert the hook in the work, wrap the yarn over the hook and draw the yarn through the work only (a) so there are now two loops on the hook, wrap the yarn again and draw the yarn through both loops on the hook (b).

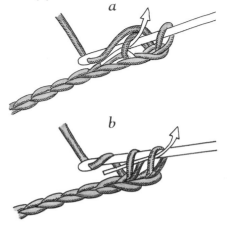

### Treble crochet (US Double crochet)

Wrap the yarn over the hook and insert the hook in the work (a), wrap the yarn over the hook and draw the yarn through the work only (b) so there are now four loops on the hook, wrap the yarn again and draw the yarn through the first two loops on the hook (c), wrap the yarn and draw the yarn through the remaining two loops on the hook (d).

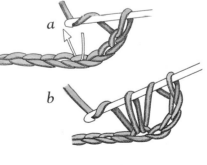

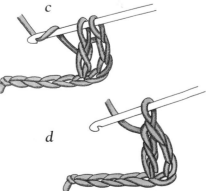

# ZANY COW

Why not knit this black and white Friesian cow? It would make an original gift for an animal lover or it could be a displayed at a country fair. You can even get your cow to 'moo' by putting an animal noisebox or growler in the centre of the cow when stuffing it.

## YOU WILL NEED
*1 pair of 4 mm (6) knitting needles*
*50 g (2-ounce skein) white double knitting yarn*
*2 stitch holders*
*Oddments of pink and black double knitting yarn*
*1 pair of 3¾ mm (5) knitting needles*
*Oddments of black double knitting chenille*
*Large darning needle*
*Scissors*
*Pins*
*Stuffing (batting)*
*Ribbon and small bell*

## TENSION (GAUGE)
Using 4 mm (6) needles, 20 sts and 24 rows to 10 cm (4 in) (st st).

## COW BODY (SIDE 1)
Using 4 mm (6) needles and white double knitting yarn, cast on 37 sts. Knitting in st st throughout, knit 2 rows.
3rd, 5th and 7th rows: inc 1 st at the end of the row.
4th, 6th and 8th rows: inc 1 st at the beg of the row. K 2 rows. K 2 tog at the end of the next and every other row until you have 37 sts. K 1 row.
Next row: k 8 sts and put them onto a stitch holder, cast (bind) off the next 17 sts, k the next 8 sts and put them onto a stitch holder. Cast (bind) off the last 4 sts. Put the 8 sts from the stitch holder back onto the needles and * k 16 rows. Change to black double knitting yarn and k 5 rows. Cast (bind) off. * Put the 8 sts on the other stitch holder onto the needles and repeat from * to *. Sew in ends.

## COW BODY (SIDE 2)
Knit as for Side 1 but reverse all shaping so that the cow body is facing in opposite direction.

## COW GUSSET (SIDE 1)
Using 4 mm (6) needles with pink and white double knitting yarn, cast on 35 pink sts and 40 white sts. Knit in st st throughout.
1st row: k 40 white sts, 35 pink sts.
2nd row: k 35 pink sts, 40 white sts.
3rd row: k 40 white sts, 35 pink sts.
4th row: cast (bind) off 6 pink sts, p 29 pink sts, 40 white sts.
5th row: cast (bind) off 6 white sts, k 34 white sts, 29 pink sts.
6th row: cast (bind) off 6 pink sts, p 23 pink sts, 34 white sts.
7th row: cast (bind) off 6 white sts, k 28 white sts, 23 pink sts.
8th row: cast (bind) off 4 pink sts, purl 19 pink sts, 28 white sts.
9th row: cast (bind) off 6 white sts, k 22 white sts, 19 pink sts.
10th row: cast (bind) off 4 pink sts, p 15 pink sts, 22 white sts.
11th row: cast (bind) off 4 white sts, k 8 white sts and put onto a stitch holder, cast (bind) off the next 10 white sts and 7 pink sts, k the last 8 pink sts.
Change to white double knitting yarn and * k 16 rows on these 8 sts. Change to black double knitting yarn and k 5 rows. Cast (bind) off.*
Put the 8 sts on the stitch holder onto the needles, rejoin white yarn and repeat from * to *. Sew in ends.

## COW GUSSET (SIDE 2)
Using 4 mm (6) needles with pink and white double knitting yarn, cast on 40 white sts and 35 pink sts. Continue as for Side 1 but reverse all shaping and placement of the pink and white yarns so that the gusset is facing in opposite direction.

## HEAD (SIDE 1)
Using 4 mm (6) needles and white double knitting yarn, cast on 18 sts. K 7 rows in st st. Cast (bind) off 2 sts at the beg of the next row.
9th, 11th and 13th rows: k 2 sts tog at the end of the row.
10th, 12th and 14th rows: k 2 tog at the beg of the row.
Cast (bind) off the 10 remaining sts. Sew in ends.

## HEAD (SIDE 2)
Knit as for Side 1 but reverse all shaping so that the head is facing in the opposite direction.

## HEAD GUSSET
Using 4 mm (6) needles and white double knitting yarn, cast on 7 sts and k 36 rows in st st. Change to pink double knitting yarn and k 8 rows. Change back to white double knitting yarn.
Next row: k 2 sts tog at the beg and end of the row. K 5 rows.
Next row: k 2 sts tog at the beg and end of the row. K 4 rows. Cast (bind) off. Sew in ends.

## EARS (knit 2 alike)
Using 4 mm (6) needles and white double knitting yarn, cast on 7 sts. K 8 rows in st st.
Next row: k 2 sts tog at the beg and end of the row. K 1 row.
Next row: k 2 sts tog at the beg and end of the row. Cast (bind) off the remaining 3 sts. Sew in ends.

## TAIL
Using 4 mm (6) needles and white double knitting yarn, cast on 6 sts. K 22 rows in st st.
Next row: k 1, k 2 tog, k 1, k 2 tog. K 5 rows. Cast (bind) off the remaining 4 sts. Sew in ends.

## UDDER (knit 4 to make up teats)
Using 4 mm (6) needles and pink double knitting yarn, cast on 5 sts. K 6 rows in st st. Break the yarn, run through the 5 sts and pull tight.

## BLACK SPOTS (knit 5)
Using 3¾ mm (5) needles and black double knitting chenille, cast on 4

sts. Knit in garter stitch throughout. K 2 rows. Inc 1 st at each end of the next row. K 2 rows. Inc 1 st at each end of the next row. K 10 rows. K 2 tog at the beg and end of the next row. K 3 rows. K 2 sts tog at the beg and end of the next row. K 1 row. Cast (bind) off the remaining 4 sts. Sew in ends.

## TO MAKE UP

### COW BODY

**1** Sew in the cow body (Side 1) to the cow gusset (Side 1) and the cow body (Side 2) to the cow gusset (Side 2). Join the cow body (Side 1) to the cow body (Side 2) along the central back seam. Join the cow gusset (Side 1) to the cow gusset (Side 2) along the pink area of the underside of cow.

### TAIL

**2** Sew up the long side seam on the tail. Make a black tassel for the end of the tail. Trim tassel to length required. Sew tail onto back end of cow body.

### UDDERS

**3** Sew up the short side seams on the teats. Sew them in place on the pink area of the cow gusset.

### HEAD

**4** Pin the head gusset around four sides of the head (Side 1), leaving the cast-off (bound-off) edge (neck edge) open. Place the widest part of the head gusset to the left-hand side of head (back of head) and sew around head so that the pink area is on the short straight edge (nose) and the narrowest part is on the right hand side of head (under cow's chin). Turn head (Side 1) and head gusset over and sew to head (Side 2). Sew the ears in place and embroider on eye and nose detail with black double knitting yarn. Stuff head and sew onto body around neck opening.

### FINISHING TOUCHES

**5** Sew on black spots. Stuff the cow, being sure to push the stuffing (batting) down into the legs using a knitting needle and stuffing the udder area well. Sew up the opening on the underside of cow. Put the bell on the ribbon and tie around the cow's neck in a bow.

# BEASTIE HAT

This hat, complete with ears, will suit any young child between the ages of 7 and 10. It is knitted in the round; if you have never done this before, this project is ideal. It is much easier than you may think and means no more sewing up or bulky seams.

## YOU WILL NEED

*4 double-pointed 3¼ mm (3) and 4 double-pointed 4 mm (6) knitting needles*
*50 g (2-ounce skein) brown double knitting (sport) yarn*
*Large darning needle*
*Scissors*
*Oddment of cream double knitting (sport) yarn*
*1 pair of 4 mm (6) knitting needles*
*Stuffing (batting)*

## TENSION (GAUGE)

Using 4 mm (6) needles, 20 sts and 24 rows to 10 cm (4 in) (st st).

## HAT

Using 3¼ mm (3) needles and brown double knitting yarn, cast on 100 sts, 33 sts on each of 1st and 2nd needles and 34 sts on 3rd needle. Work 10 rounds in k 1, p 1 rib. Work should measure 5 cm (2 in).
Change to 4 mm (6) needles and k 14 rounds (st st).
Shape crown as follows:
1st round: k 8, k 2 tog 10 times round (90 sts).
2nd and every alternate round: k the round.
3rd round: k 7, k 2 tog 10 times round (80 sts).
5th round: k 6, k 2 tog 10 times round (70 sts).

Continue dec thus until 20 sts remain. K 1 round.
Next round: k 2 tog 10 times round (10 sts). Break yarn, thread through remaining sts, draw up tightly and fasten off securely. Sew in the ends.

## EARS

### BACK (knit 2 alike)
Using 4 mm (6) needles and brown double knitting yarn, cast on 14 sts. K 6 rows in st st. K 2 tog at beg and end of the next and following 4th row. K 1 row. K 2 sts tog at the beginning and end of the next three rows. Cast (bind) off the remaining 4 sts. Sew in the ends.

### FRONT (knit 2 alike)
Using brown double knitting yarn and cream double knitting yarn, knit as for back, following chart for colour changes. Sew in the ends.

## TO MAKE UP

Pin ear fronts to ear backs (with wrong sides together). Using the brown yarn, oversew the pieces together leaving the bottom edge open. Stuff and sew in place on top of the hat.

# PRAM TOYS

These simple, geometric pram toys are the perfect project for a beginner or child to knit. They are also a good way to use up oddments of yarn. If they do not keep the baby happy, you could add a little seasonal embroidery and quickly turn them into unusual Christmas decorations.

## YOU WILL NEED

*Scraps of brightly coloured double knitting yarn*
*1 pair of 4 mm (6) knitting needles*
*Scissors*
*Tape measure*
*Pins*
*Large darning needle*
*Stuffing (batting)*
*Flat plastic squeakers or small bells*

## TENSION (GAUGE)
This will differ according to the yarn used.

*SQUARE (knit 2 alike)*
Using 4 mm (6) needles, cast on 15 sts. K 18 rows in st st. Cast (bind) off. Sew in ends.

*TRIANGLE (knit 2 alike)*
Using 4 mm (6) needles, cast on 20 sts. K 2 rows in st st. K 2 tog at the beg and end of the next and every other row until 2 sts remain. K these 2 sts tog and pass the yarn through the last st. Sew in the ends.

*DIAMOND (knit 2 alike)*
Using 4 mm (6) needles, cast on 2 sts. K 2 rows in st st. Inc 1 st at the beg and end of the next and every other row until you have 14 sts. P 1 row. K 2 sts tog at the beg and end of the next and every other row until you have 2 sts. P 1 row. Cast (bind) off. Sew in the ends.

## TO MAKE UP

**1** Cut three 20 cm (8 in) lengths of yarn, knot together and plait (braid) to make the hanging loop. Knot the ends to fasten. Pin two matching shapes together (with wrong sides together). Place the hanging loop at the centre top with the ends between the two sides. Sew the shapes together, stitching down the hanging loop at the same time and leaving a gap of 5 cm (2 in) for stuffing (batting).

**2** Stuff lightly, placing a flat plastic squeaker or bell in the centre of each toy. Sew up the gap.

The simple ribbed scarf is given a designer touch, being finished off with glittering pompons. The mittens, although knitted in the round, are very quick and simple to knit. As the thumb shaping is worked on the side, one mitten fits either hand. The set will fit 10–12 years.

## YOU WILL NEED

For scarf:
*1 pair of 4 mm (6) knitting needles*
*250 g (8-ounce skein) double knitting yarn*
*60 m (65 yds) metallic yarn*
*Tape measure*
*Stiff card*
For mittens:
*4 double-pointed 4 mm (6) knitting needles*
*50 g (2-ounce skein) double knitting yarn*
*Stitch holder*
*Large darning needle*
*Scissors*

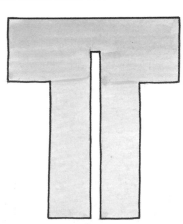

### SCARF

## TENSION (GAUGE)

Using 4 mm (6) needles, 38 sts and 28 rows to 10 cm (4 in) (k 2, p 2 rib).
Using 4 mm (6) needles and double knitting yarn, cast on 64 sts. Work in k 2, p 2 rib throughout. When scarf measures 130 cm (50 in) cast (bind) off. Sew in ends.

## TO MAKE UP

### TO MAKE POMPONS

**1** Trace the template, draw it onto very stiff card and cut out. Wind the double knitting yarn and the metallic yarn around the narrower area of card together until the yarn is 15 mm (⅝ in) deep.

**2** Tie a piece of yarn tightly around the centre of the pompon. Cut the yarn either side of the card to release the pompon from the card template, and trim until the pompon is neat and round.

**3** Using metallic yarn mixed in with the double knitting yarn, make 6 medium-sized pompons. Sew 3 onto each end of the scarf, 1 on each corner and 1 in the centre.

### MITTENS *(knit 2 alike)*

## TENSION (GAUGE)

Using 4 mm (6) needles, 20 sts and 25 rows to 10 cm (4 in) (st st).
Using set of 4 double-pointed 4 mm (6) needles and double knitting yarn, cast on 36 sts, 12 sts on each of the 3 needles.
Work 11 rounds in k 2, p 2 rib.
Next round: rib 8, inc in the next st knitways, rib 8, inc in the next st knitways, rib 7, inc in the next st knitways, rib 7, inc in the next st knitways, rib 2 (40 sts).
K 14 rounds.
Next round: k the first 8 sts and put them onto a stitch holder. Cast on 8 extra sts, k them and the rest of the round. K 12 rounds.
Shaping mittens:
1st round: k 3, k 2 tog, k 18, k 2 tog, k 15.
2nd round: k 2, k 2 tog, k 17, k 2 tog, k 15.
3rd round: k 1, k 2 tog, k 16, k 2 tog, k 15.
4th round: k 2, k 15, k 2 tog, k 14, k

the last st of this round and the first st of the next round tog.

5th round: k 14, k 2 tog, k 13, k the last st of this round and the first st of the next round tog.

6th round: k 13, k 2 tog, k 12, k the last st of this round and the first st of the next round tog.

7th round: k 12, k 2 tog, k 11, k the last st of this round and the first st of the next round tog.

8th round: k 11, k 2 tog, k 10, k the last st of this round and the first st of the next round tog.

9th round: k 10, k 2 tog, k 9, k the last st of this round and the first st of the next round tog.

10th round: k 9, k 2 tog, k 9, k 2 tog. Cast (bind) off the remaining 20 st.

## THUMB
Pick up the 8 sts cast at the thumb and then put them, together with the 8 sts from the stitch holder, onto the needles, 5 sts on each of the 1st and 2nd needles and 6 sts on 3rd needle. K 12 rounds. Cast (bind) off by k 2 sts tog until 2 sts remain. Break the yarn and run it through these 2 sts.

## TO MAKE UP
Sew up the gap at the top of each mitten and sew in all the ends.

# CHILD'S BAG

This child's bag is made up of various different-shaped rectangles knitted in garter stitch and decorated with French knitting. It is an ideal project for a child although an adult's help will be required for the sewing up. It could easily be converted into a shoulder bag by simply knitting longer handles.

## YOU WILL NEED
*100 g (4-ounce skein) bright green aran-weight wool*
*100 g (4-ounce skein) bright orange double knitting (sport) yarn*
*1 pair of 5 mm (8) knitting needles*
*French knitting doll (knitting knobby)*
*Large darning needle*
*Scissors*
*Tape measure*

## TENSION (GAUGE)
Using 5 mm (8) needles, 14 sts and 28 rows to 10 cm (4 in) (garter stitch).

## BODY OF BAG
Using 5 mm (8) needles and green aran-weight wool, cast on 28 sts. K 94 rows in garter stitch. Cast (bind) off.

## BAG BASE
Using 5 mm (8) needles and green aran-weight wool, cast on 14 sts. K 24 rows in garter stitch. Cast (bind) off.

## HANDLES (knit 2 alike)
Using 5 mm (8) needles and green aran-weight wool, cast on 6 sts. K 56 rows in garter stitch. Cast (bind) off.

## LOOPS
Using a French knitting doll (knitting knobby), make 100 g (4-ounce skein) orange double knitting yarn into a length of knitted tube.

## TO MAKE UP
Fold the body of the bag in half so that the knitting is sideways and sew the cast-on edge to the cast-off (bound-off) edge. Sew the base onto the body. Turn the bag right-side out so the seams are on the inside. Turn the top of the bag down 5 cm (2 in) to form a brim. Sew in place. Fold the bag in half, keeping the base square, and sew one handle onto one side of the bag on the folded top edge, leaving a 4 cm (1½ in) gap between the handle ends. Repeat on the other side. Sew in all ends.

## SEWING DOWN LOOPS
Sew one end of the knitted tube to the body of the bag just under the brim. Fold over to form a loop 5 cm (2 in) long and sew the tube down 15 mm (⅝ in) away from the other end of loop. Repeat this down the length of the bag. When you reach the base, turn and come back up the length of the bag, stopping at the base of the brim. Continue zigzagging up and down the bag making loops until the whole bag is covered, spacing the rows of loops about 2.5 cm (1 in) apart.

*Knitting & Crochet*

# CHRISTMAS BAUBLES

Brighten up the Christmas tree with these bright baubles. Any oddments will do and you can vary the colour schemes according to the yarns you have.

## YOU WILL NEED
*Oddments of 4-ply glitter yarn*
*3.0 mm (D) and 3.5 mm (E) crochet*
*    hooks*
*Polystyrene balls*
*Non-toxic gold craft paint*
*Small paintbrush*
*Tapestry needle*

## MEASUREMENTS
The bauble circle should measure 13 cm (5¼ in) in diameter.

## BAUBLE PATTERN
Using the first colour, make 3 ch and join into a ring with a ss into first ch.
Round 1: 3 ch 15 tr into ring, join with a ss into the top of first ch.
Round 2: 3 ch 2 tr into each tr to end. Break off first colour and join in the second colour with a ss into top of first ch.
Round 3: 3 ch *2 tr into next tr, 1 tr; repeat from * around, join with a ss into first ch.
Round 4: 3 ch *tr into first tr, 2 tr; repeat from * around, join with a ss into first ch.
Round 5: 3 ch *tr into first tr 3 tr; repeat from * around, join with a ss into first ch.
Round 6: 3 ch *tr into first tr, 4 tr, repeat from * around, join with a ss into first ch. Fasten off, leaving a long piece of yarn.

## HANGING LOOP
With the 3.0 mm (D) hook and the first colour, make 40 ch or a number of ch 40 cm (15½ in) long. Join with a ss into first ch. Fasten off.

## TO MAKE UP
1 Paint the polystyrene balls with gold craft paint. It may be easier to paint one half of the ball and leave it to dry before continuing with the other half.

2 Thread the long piece of yarn left on the bauble circle through a tapestry needle and run a gathering stitch all the way around the outer edge of the crocheted piece.

Place the ball in the centre of the crocheted circle. Pull on the length of yarn to gather the circle up around the ball. Fasten at the top. Attach the loop to the top of the bauble.

# BABY SHAWL

This delightful shawl is perfect for very young babies. Made in cotton, it is ideal for the summer as well as being a cosy indoor wrap in the cooler months. Its delicate repeated pattern suits both boys and girls equally well.

## YOU WILL NEED
*450 g (1 lb) 4-ply cotton*
*2.5 mm (C) crochet hook*

## MEASUREMENTS
112 cm (44 in) square.
Make a number of chains divisible by 5 plus 1, 3 turning ch. The chain should measure 112 cm (44 in).

## LACE PATTERN
Base row: work 1 dttr in 4th ch from hook, miss 4 ch, * 5 dttr in next ch, miss 4 ch. Rep from * to end of row ending with 3 dttr in last ch, 4 turning ch.
Row 1: 2 dttr in first st, * 5 dttr in centre st of shell. Rep from * to end of row ending with 2 dttr in turning ch, 4 turning ch.
Row 2: 1 dttr in first st, *5 dttr in centre st of shell. Rep from * to end of row ending with 3 dttr in turning ch, 4 turning ch.

Rep rows 1 and 2 until the shawl measures 112 cm (44 in). Fasten off.

## EDGING
This is worked all the way around the outside of the shawl piece. With the right side of the work facing, attach the yarn to one edge.
1dc into same place * 3 ch, 1 ss into last dc formed. 1 dc into each of next 3 sts. Rep from * to end omitting 1 dc at end of last rep, ss into first dc. Fasten off.

# CLEVER CAMOUFLAGE

Just the thing to add a decorative touch to the bathroom, and disguise the toilet paper roll. You can alter the colours of the cover to match the bathroom suite.

## YOU WILL NEED

*40 g (1½ oz) cream 4-ply mercerized cotton*
*Oddments of 4-ply cotton for flowers*
*2.5 mm (C) crochet hook*
*Iron*
*Soft cloth*
*Tapestry needle*

## MEASUREMENTS FOR BASE

40.5 cm (16 in) in width; 15 cm (6 in) in height.

## BASE

Make a ch 40.5 cm (16 in) long, plus 3 turning ch.
Row 1: Work 1 tr into third ch from hook. Work 1 tr into each ch to end, turn with 3 ch.
Row 2: Work 1 tr into each tr to end, turn with 3 ch. Repeat row 2 until work measures 15 cm (6 in). Fasten off.

## FLOWERS

Make a total of 13 flowers.
Made 8 ch and join into a ring with a ss into first ch.
Round 1: 6 ch *1 tr in ring, 3 ch; repeat from * 4 more times, 1 ss into third of 6 ch.
Round 2: Into each space work 1 dc, 1 htr, 3 tr, 1 htr, and 1 dc: this forms 6 petals.
Round 3: * 5 ch, 1 dc into next tr of round before last, inserting hook from back; repeat from * ending with 5 ch.
Round 4: Into each space work 1 dc, 1 htr, 5 tr, 1 htr, 5 tr, 1 htr and 1 dc.
Round 5: *7 ch, 1 dc into next dc of round before last, inserting hook from back; repeat from * ending with 7 ch.

Round 6: Into each space work 1 dc, 1 htr, 7 tr, 1 htr and 1 c, 1 ss into first dc. Fasten off.

## TO MAKE UP

Press the base on the wrong side using a warm iron over a damp cloth. Place all the flowers apart from the central top one and stitch down using a tapestry needle. Fold the base in half with the rights sides together and stitch along the seam. Fasten off leaving a long piece of yarn. Thread the remaining piece of yarn through the tapestry needle and run a gathering stitch all round the top edge. Gather up and fasten off. Stitch down the remaining flower.

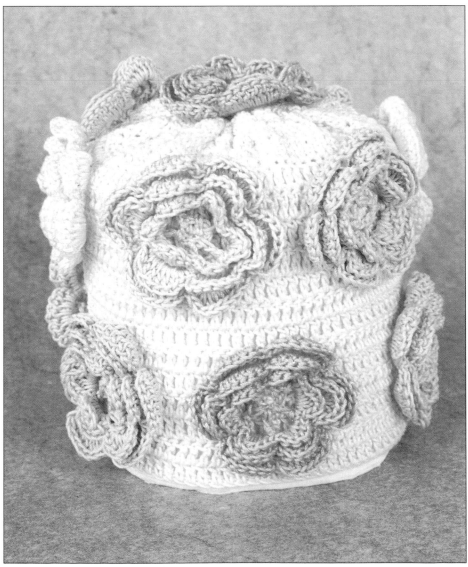

# EGG COSIES

Keep your breakfast eggs warm and looking cheerful with these bright cosies. Simply pop them over the eggs in their cups and they will welcome the whole family to the table!

## YOU WILL NEED
*Oddments of coloured 4-ply cotton*
*4.0 mm (F) crochet hook*
*3.0 mm (D) crochet hook*
*Damp cloth*
*Steam iron*
*Needle*

## COSIES
Using the 4.0 mm (F) hook make 32 ch.
Work 1 tr into 2nd ch from hook, work 1 tr into each ch to end. Turn with 3 ch.
Next row: work 1 tr into each tr to end, turn with 3 ch.
Rep the last row 5 times more, then dec 6 sts evenly over the next row.
Next row: work in tr, missing every alternate st. Fasten off.

## LOOP
Using the 3.0 mm (D) hook, make 12 ch.
Work 1 dc into each ch, join with an ss. Fasten off.

## TO MAKE UP
Cover the cosies with a damp cloth and press using a warm iron. Stitch along the side seam. Run a gathering stitch along the top and pull to gather. Sew the loop to the top of the cosy.

# PRETTY PILLOW EDGING

This lace braid can be made up in varying lengths to trim all manner of pillows or cushions. Measure the total outside edges of the pillowcase or cushion cover and continue crocheting until you have enough to go all the way round.

## YOU WILL NEED
*50 g (2 oz) 4-ply mercerized cotton*
*2.5 mm (C) crochet hook*
*Steam iron*
*Soft cloth*
*Needle and thread*

## MEASUREMENTS
Use a number of chains divisible by 5 plus 3.

### LACE EDGING PATTERN
Row 1: miss one ch * 1 dc into each ch; rep from * to end of row. Turn.
Row 2: ss into first dc * 3 ch, miss 3 dc, ss into next 2 dc. Rep from * to end of row. Turn.
Row 3: ss into first st 2 ss * (1 tr, 1 ch) 4 times in next 2 ss. Rep from * to end of row. Fasten off.

## TO MAKE UP
Press the braid lightly on the wrong side with a warm iron over a damp cloth. Take care not to stretch the braid when pressing. Sew the braid onto the pillowcase or cushion cover.

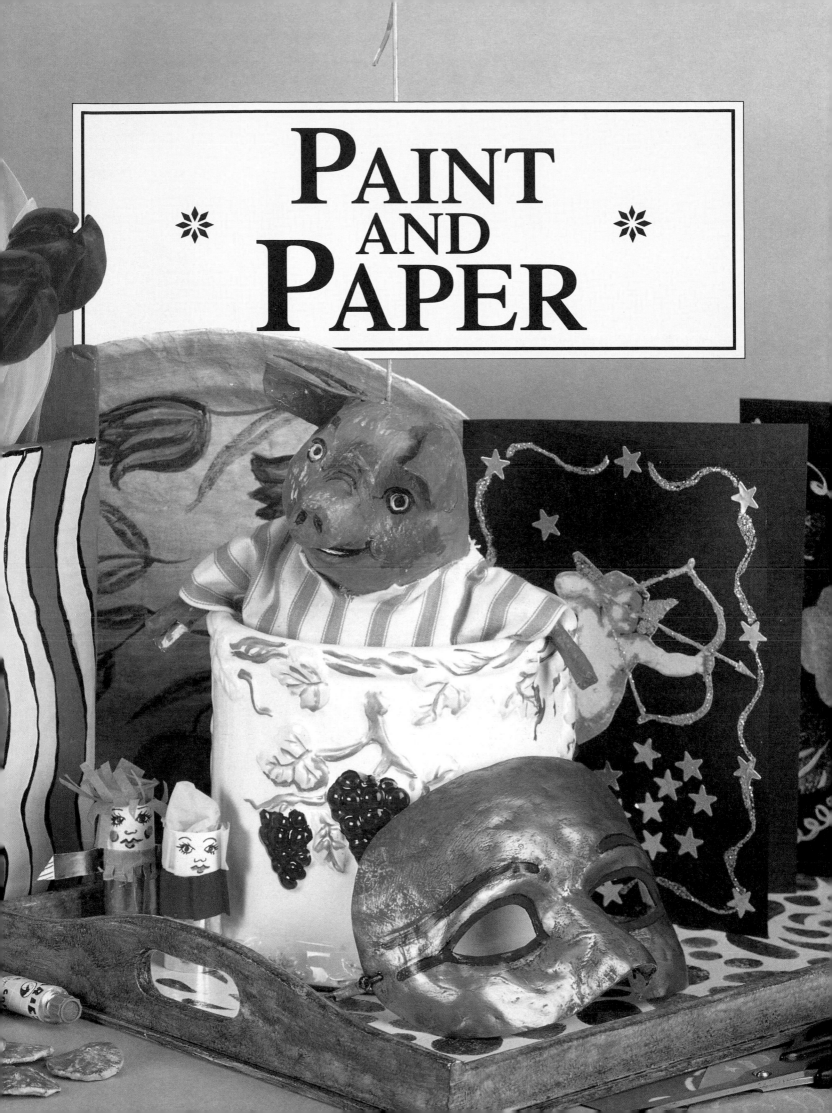

# PAINT AND PAPER

# PAPIER-MÂCHÉ TECHNIQUES

## Materials

Papier-mâché is the art of modelling with torn or shredded paper bound together with glue, usually a water-based variety. The skills of papier-mâché are very quick to master and offer endless variation. Only readily-available materials and equipment are required: newspaper or coloured craft paper, glue, large bowls or dishes, and masking tape. The most convenient adhesive to bind papier-mâché is PVA glue. This is non-toxic and can be diluted with water to give different strengths. It dries very quickly to leave a strong surface that will hold paint well.

## Shredding paper

Old newspapers are excellent for papier-mâché. Tear them along the grain of the paper – the direction in which tearing is easiest – into strips approximately 2.5-5 cm (1-2 in) wide. Do not worry about creating ragged edges when you tear as these give a smoother finish to the object. Coloured papers can also be used, and give a decorative mosaic effect. Tear an assortment of colours into rough squares, approximately 2.5 cm (1 in) in size. The colours can be alternated when glued down. Again, rough edges are an advantage, both in producing a smooth finish and in creating a pleasantly mottled appearance.

## Moulds and frameworks

Almost any object can be used as a mould for papier-mâché, although rounded surfaces are easier to cover smoothly if the mould is to be removed later. Bowls or large dishes are excellent and one side can be covered to create a replica of the shape. Covering an inflated balloon creates a useful spherical mould. When the papier-mâché is dry, pop the balloon with a pin and remove the rubber through the opening left at the bottom of the mould.

Before applying papier-mâché to a mould, ensure it is first greased with a liberal coating of petroleum jelly (*above*) so that it can be removed easily when dry.

Papier-mâché can also be constructed without using a mould. This method is particularly useful for making jewellery or buttons. Squash lumps of glue-soaked paper into shapes between your fingers. To pierce holes in buttons or beads, carefully push a fine knitting needle or kitchen skewer through the wet paper and leave to dry.

## Building up the shape

Soak the pieces of paper one by one as you need them in diluted PVA glue. If covering a mould or framework (*left*), lay on the strips individually, working from top to bottom of the shape, with the strips

running in the same direction. When the first layer is complete, apply another, this time running in the opposite direction. This provides extra strength. Apply about four layers in all, more if you want your construction to be particularly strong. As a final touch, it may be useful to brush a coat of glue over the layers using a large paintbrush.

For added decoration or extra detail, add scrunched up balls of paper soaked in glue. These may need a little extra adhesive support from small pieces of masking tape to hold them in place. Cover with a layer of paper soaked in glue for a smooth finish.

## Drying

When modelling is complete, leave the papier-mâché to dry thoroughly. Leave in a warm place such as an airing cupboard, preferably overnight. Do not leave near a direct heat source as this may cause the papier-mâché to bend and warp.

## Decoration

When the papier-mâché is dry, gently remove the mould, if one has been used. If you want a neat finish, trim and re-cover the rough edges where the paper pieces overlapped (*above*). Sometimes, however, these uneven finishes can be very decorative, on the rim of a bowl for example.

If you are painting your object, prime with two coats of white paint, leaving the first coat to dry before applying the second. This will conceal any newsprint that may show through the colours. Both poster paints and acrylics are ideal for colouring papier-mâché (*right*), and all types of decoration can be applied from freehand designs, sponging and stippling to the addition of 'gems' and metallic braid.

To give papier-mâché a shiny finish and added strength it can be coated with clear non-toxic varnish.

Remember that, although papier-mâché objects are both highly decorative and fully functional, they are not watertight: vases and bowls should be used to hold dried flowers or nuts and fruit rather than fresh bouquets or liquids.

# CROWN BOX

This regal box with its golden crowns would be perfect for holding cufflinks or earrings. Bigger boxes could, of course, be made for larger items — perhaps envelopes and writing paper, or paintbrushes.

## YOU WILL NEED

*Tracing paper*
*Pencil*
*Ruler*
*Heavy corrugated cardboard*
*Craft knife*
*Strong clear glue*
*Masking tape*
*Newspaper*
*Diluted PVA glue*
*Fine sandpaper*
*Small paintbrush*
*Assorted poster paints*
*Clear gloss varnish*

**1** Scale up the templates for the box pieces and transfer them to the heavy cardboard.

Cut out each piece with a craft knife. Glue the pieces together, and tape them in place.

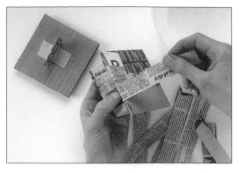

**2** Tear the newspaper into strips about 2.5 cm (1 in) wide. Fill a bowl with diluted PVA glue. Dip each strip of paper into the glue and stick it down onto the box framework.

Overlap each strip of paper slightly, to give added strength. Cover both parts of the box with four layers of papier-mâché, and leave to dry in a warm place.

**3** When the box is dry, lightly smooth its surface with fine sandpaper

and prime it with two coats of white paint. Draw in the crown motifs.

**4** Decorate the box with poster or gouache paints. You may wish to

add definition to the design with black paint.

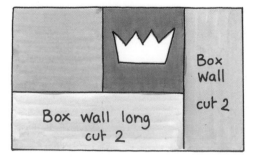

**5** Allow the box to dry overnight, and then seal

it with two coats of clear gloss varnish. Leave to dry.

| | | Box Wall cut 2 |
|---|---|---|
| Box wall long cut 2 | | |

# WALL SCONCE

Make this bright wall container to cheer up a corner of the kitchen. Its very simple design could be easily adapted to hold a variety of things, and it could of course be decorated to suit your own colour scheme.

## YOU WILL NEED

*Tracing paper*
*Pencil*
*Ruler*
*Heavy corrugated cardboard*
*Craft knife*
*Strong clear glue*
*Masking tape*
*Newspaper*
*Diluted PVA glue*
*Fine sandpaper*
*Assorted poster paints*
*Small paintbrush*
*Clear gloss varnish*
*Metal hanger*

**1** Scale up the templates and transfer each piece of the wall sconce to heavy corrugated cardboard. Be sure to make two side pieces! Cut out each piece of the wall sconce with a craft knife.

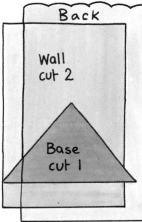

Back

Wall
cut 2

Base
cut 1

**2** Glue and tape the sconce together. Tear newspaper into strips about 2.5 cm (1 in) wide. Dip each strip of paper into diluted PVA glue and then lay it onto the sconce, slightly overlapping the previous one to give added strength. Repeat this process until you have covered the sconce. You may not be able to cover the inside completely — go down as far as you can. Apply three layers of papier-mâché. Allow to dry overnight.

**3** Smooth the surface lightly with fine sandpaper, and prime it with two coats of white paint. When dry, draw on your design in pencil.

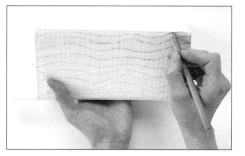

**4** Start filling in the design with poster paint. You may wish to use black paint to add definition to the design.

**5** Allow the paint to dry thoroughly, and then seal the sconce with two coats of clear gloss varnish. When dry, stick the metal hanger to the back with strong clear glue.

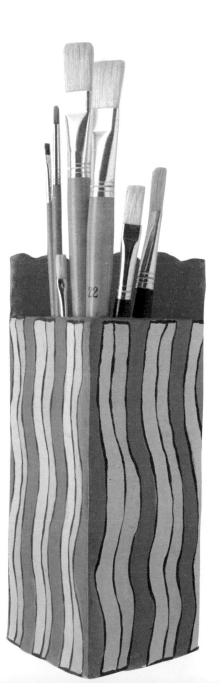

# BUTTONS

If you have ever had difficulty finding just the right buttons for a hand-knitted garment, or hated the plastic ones on a jacket, then papier-mâché buttons could be the solution! Make a simple, brightly coloured set like this one, or be really adventurous and use miniature confectionery moulds to produce exotically shaped buttons.

## YOU WILL NEED
*Newspaper*
*Diluted PVA glue*
*Scissors*
*Fine sandpaper*
*Assorted poster paints*
*Small paintbrush*
*Darning needle*
*Clear gloss varnish*

**1** Tear the newspaper into long strips about 2.5 cm (1 in) wide. Fill a bowl with diluted PVA glue and dip a strip of paper into the glue. Allow it to soak for a few seconds, and then roughly shape it into a flat circle. Squash the circle firmly between your finger and thumb, and leave it to dry in a warm place. Make as many buttons as required.

**2** Trim each dry button into a neat circle. Tear some small, thin strips of newspaper, dip into the diluted PVA glue and use to bind the edges of each button. Allow the buttons to dry.

**3** Smooth the surface of each button lightly with fine sandpaper, and then apply two coats of white paint. Colour the buttons with poster paint. The mottled effect is achieved by using three uneven coats of paint, each coat being a couple of shades darker than the previous one.

**4** Use a darning needle to make two or four regularly spaced holes in each button.

**5** Seal the surface of each button with two coats of clear gloss varnish.

# PRETTY PLATTER

This ornamental and practical platter can be used on special occasions, and is pretty enough to display in your kitchen at other times. Do remember not to wash it; just clean it by wiping it with a damp cloth.

## YOU WILL NEED
*Platter for a mould*
*Petroleum jelly*
*Newspaper*
*Wallpaper paste*
*Craft knife*
*White matt emulsion paint*
*Large paintbrush*
*Small paintbrush*
*Assorted poster paints*
*Pencil*
*Clear gloss varnish*

**1** Grease the platter with a layer of petroleum jelly. Cover the platter with at least six layers of newspaper strips soaked in wallpaper paste. Leave an overlap of 20 mm (¾ in) around the edge. Leave to dry in a warm place for at least 3 days.

**2** Trim the edges with a craft knife and remove the papier-mâché shape from the platter. Do not use any force; it separates easily when it is completely dry.

Cover the edges with two layers of papier-mâché for a neat finish. Leave to dry, then prime the platter with two coats of white matt emulsion paint and leave to dry.

**3** Cover the platter with a thin wash of colour and leave to dry.

**4** Decorate by drawing the design onto the platter in pencil, and then very carefully paint in the design.

**5** Allow the paint to dry, and then seal it with two coats of clear gloss varnish. Leave to dry overnight in a warm place.

# PIGLET PUPPET

Children will love this appealing puppet which is made from inexpensive materials. Piglet's head is easy to sculpt in papier-mâché. A whole farmyard of animals can be constructed in the same way.

## YOU WILL NEED
*Wire coat hanger*
*Small plastic yogurt pot*
*Masking tape*
*Newspaper*
*Stiff paper*
*Small mixing bowl*
*Diluted PVA glue*
*Rubber-covered wire*
*Poster paint*
*Round paintbrush*
*Flat paintbrush*
*Scissors*
*45 cm × 30 cm (18 in × 12 in) fabric*

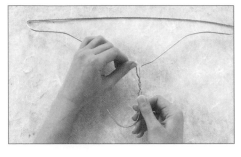

**1** Untwist a wire coat hanger and straighten it into a long length.

**2** Make a circular base of the wire at one end. Use the remaining wire as a backbone and bend the other end into a long hook. Make a hole in the centre of the base of the yogurt pot, and slide it down over the hook until it is about 16 cm (6½ in) above the base. Secure with masking tape, and stuff it with newspaper.

**3** Wrap strips of newspaper about 20 mm (¾ in) wide around the yogurt pot to form the head. Roll a small strip of stiff paper into a cylinder to form the snout and tape on.

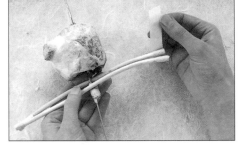

**4** Form cheeks of small balls of newspaper and attach to the head with masking tape. Dip strips of newspaper into the PVA glue and wrap them around head. Build up four layers of strips. Leave to dry overnight.

**5** Cut two equal short lengths of rubber-covered wire. Bind the ends together with masking tape to form trotters. Tape onto the wire just beneath the head.

**6** Cut out two ears from stiff paper and tape onto the head. Paint the head and hooves a pink pig colour, and add the details of the features. Leave to dry.

**7** Cut out the robe in one piece and spread glue along the edges of the material. Make a hole for the head. Pull the robe over the pig's head, and the sleeves over the 'arms'.

# EGYPTIAN MASK

Create this beautiful mask at home using professional mask makers' techniques which allow a perfect fit. You will be surprised at how easily you can produce new identities for all your friends and family.

## YOU WILL NEED
*Old scarf*
*Petroleum jelly*
*Paper tissues*
*Gummed brown paper tape*
*Black felt-tip pen*
*Diluted PVA glue*
*Large paintbrush*
*Scissors*
*Assorted poster paints*
*Small paintbrush*
*Fine sandpaper*
*Gilt wax*
*Soft cloth*
*Elastic*

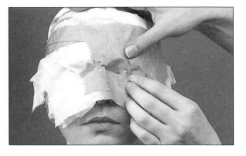

**1** Ask the model to sit in a relaxed position. Cover the hair with an old scarf. Apply a liberal covering of petroleum jelly to the face, especially on and around the nose, eyes and eyebrows. Cover the face and eyelids with a thin layer of paper tissues.

**2** Tear off strips of gummed paper tape. Make a band that passes around the forehead and fasten in place by moistening the paper. Soak small pieces of tape in water and apply them to the model's face on top of the tissues. Begin at the forehead and work down, making sure the pieces overlap slightly. Add two more layers. Smooth out any air bubbles. Cut the back of the headband and gently lift the mask away. Leave to dry overnight.

**3** Coat the mask with a layer of diluted PVA glue and allow to dry. Repeat twice. Gently replace the mask on the model's head and hold in place with a vertical band of gummed paper. Draw eyeshapes around and slightly larger than the eyes with a black felt-tip pen. Take care not to go too close to the eye sockets. Gently remove the mask from the model.

**4** Cut out the eye shapes. Paint the mask with white paint and sand down when dry. Paint the mask a deep red and again leave to dry.

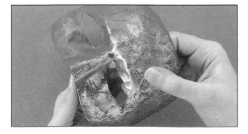

**5** Rub on a thin coat of gilt wax with a cloth, allowing the red to show through. Buff the gold using your thumb and paint a blue outline around the eyes. Make holes on the sides of the mask, thread elastic and knot.

# DESIGNER BOWL

Small pieces of blue, yellow and orange paper were used to create this striking papier-mâché bowl. Try combining other colours of your choice.

## YOU WILL NEED
*Glass bowl*
*Petroleum jelly*
*Brightly coloured paper*
*Diluted PVA glue*
*Scissors*
*Large paintbrush*

**1** Cover the inside of a glass bowl with a layer of petroleum jelly.

**2** Tear the paper into many pieces about 2.5 cm (1 in) large. Soak a few pieces of paper at a time in the diluted PVA glue. Press against the inside of the bowl, slightly overlapping each piece. Cover the whole bowl. Add a second layer, and repeat the process four or five times. Leave to dry in a warm place.

**3** When the papier-mâché is thoroughly dry, remove from the bowl.

**4** Touch up if necessary with more glue-soaked pieces of paper and trim the top to leave a wavy edge. Leave to dry. Finish with a clear coat of diluted PVA glue.

# EARRINGS AND BROOCH SET

This dazzling set would make a lovely Christmas present – especially in these jewel-like colours! The earring backs, brooch clip and head pins are known as 'findings' and are available from hobby and craft suppliers, as well as theatrical costumiers.

## YOU WILL NEED

*Heavy corrugated cardboard*
*Pair of compasses*
*Pencil*
*Craft knife*
*Newspaper*
*Diluted PVA glue*
*Fine sandpaper*
*White and gold acrylic paint*
*Small paintbrush*
*Strong clear glue*
*Glass 'gems' and small beads*
*Darning needle*
*9 headpins*
*Pair of earring backs*
*Brooch clip*

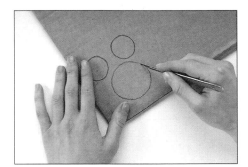

**1** Draw two 2.5 cm (1 in) circles and one 5 cm (2 in) circle on heavy cardboard, and cut out with a craft knife.

**2** Tear newspaper into strips about 6–12 mm (¼–½ in) wide. Fill a bowl with diluted PVA glue. Dip each strip of paper into the glue, and apply to the brooch and earring pieces. The paper strips should overlap slightly, to add strength to the pieces. Cover each with four layers of papier-mâché. Allow to dry overnight in a warm place.

**3** Smooth the jewellery pieces lightly with fine sandpaper, and then prime each with two coats of white paint. When they are dry, decorate with two coats of gold paint.

**4** Stick the glass 'gems' to the front of each earring, and the brooch. Make three holes in the bottom of each piece with a darning needle. Fix a hanging bead onto the top of each headpin, dab a spot of glue around each hole, and push the stems of the headpins in place. Stick the brooch clip and earring backs in place with strong clear glue.

# VASE

This light, strong vase is not waterproof but an arrangement of dried or artificial flowers would look very striking in it. Other shapes and designs can be created by adapting this idea.

## YOU WILL NEED
Heavy corrugated cardboard
Pencil
Craft knife
Plain paper
Masking tape
Clear glue
Diluted PVA glue
Newspaper
White matt emulsion paint
Large paintbrush
Fine sandpaper
Coloured chalk
Small paintbrush
Gouache paints
Clear polyurethane varnish

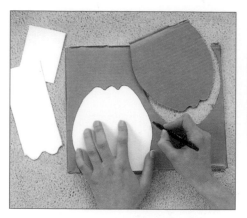

**1** Scale up the template and use to cut out the vase shapes from heavy corrugated cardboard.

**2** Using masking tape and clear glue, construct the vase leaving the front open. Coat all the pieces with diluted PVA glue to strengthen the vase. Allow these to dry for 3–4 hours. Shred newspaper into strips, and soak in diluted PVA. Cover all the pieces with four layers of papier mâché. Leave to dry in a warm place for about 12 hours. Prime the inside of the vase with two coats of white matt emulsion paint and leave to dry.

**3** Use clear glue and masking tape to stick the front onto the vase. Cover the joins with four layers of papier mâché. Leave to dry, then rub down with fine sandpaper. Paint with two coats of matt white emulsion and again leave to dry.

**4** Draw a motif onto a piece of paper. Chalk the back of this design using coloured chalk. Place the chalked paper on the front of the vase, securing it with masking tape. Draw over the design with a pencil, then remove the paper carefully. Draw over the chalk imprint lightly with the pencil. Cover the vase with a coloured paint wash. Paint in the shapes using gouache. Leave to dry. Seal with two coats of clear polyurethane varnish.

# TRINKET DISH

This trinket dish takes its inspiration from Celtic metalwork. Although the design is simple, it is very effective and bright.

## YOU WILL NEED

*Bowl to use as a mould*
*Petroleum jelly*
*Newspaper*
*Diluted PVA glue*
*Scissors*
*Fine sandpaper*
*White and gold acrylic paint*
*Small paintbrush*
*Glass 'gems'*
*Strong clear glue*

**1** Grease the inside of the bowl lightly with petroleum jelly to allow easy removal of the papier-mâché when dry. Tear newspaper into strips about 2.5 cm (1 in) wide. Fill a bowl with diluted PVA glue and dip a strip of paper into it. Lay the glued paper into the greased bowl, and smooth it gently into the curves. Lay a second strip of paper so that it slightly covers the first, and continue until the inside of the bowl is completely covered. Repeat the process until you have completed four layers of papier-mâché, and then leave to dry overnight in a warm place.

**2** When the papier-mâché is dry, remove it carefully from the mould. Trim the edges of the paper shape, and bind them with short, narrow strips of newspaper which have been dipped in the bowl of diluted PVA glue. Let the papier-mâché dish dry thoroughly.

**3** Smooth the bowl lightly with fine sandpaper, and prime it with two coats of white paint. Apply two coats of gold paint and allow to dry thoroughly.

**4** Fix the glass 'gems' to the bowl using strong clear glue. Space the stones evenly, and use a variety of colours.

# WHIRLING WINDMILL

Small children never cease to be fascinated by a windmill. The ribbon hides the straw as well as being decorative. You can use any combination of colours; try winding two different colours of ribbon around the straw.

## YOU WILL NEED
*Pencil*
*Ruler*
*Square of stiff paper*
*Scissors*
*Map pin*
*Empty ballpoint pen ink cartridge*
*Plastic drinking straw*
*Disc of cork*
*Ribbon*

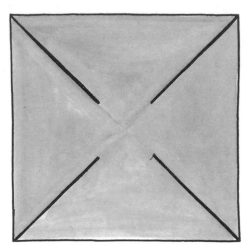

**1** Scale up the pattern from the template and transfer it onto a square of stiff paper. Cut along the lines from each corner 7.5 cm (3 in) into the centre. Make a pin hole in alternate points and curl these over to the centre.

**2** Push the map pin through all four points in the centre to the back of the windmill shape.

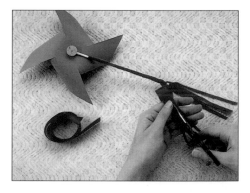

**3** Use a small piece cut from the end of an empty ballpoint pen ink cartridge as a bearing to enable the windmill to turn. Fit it over the point of the pin and then push the pin through a drinking straw. To stop the pin protruding and to secure it, push the point into a disc of cork. Wind a long piece of ribbon up the length of the straw, leaving a gap of about 3 cm (1¼ in) at the top so that the windmill can turn freely. Then wind the ribbon back down to the bottom and finish with a neat knot, leaving a loose piece at the end. Make four small cuts in the loose end to fringe.

# BOOK MARK

Are you always losing your place in the book you are reading? Keep track of your place in a favourite book, piece of music or collection of fairy tales with this lively and appealing book mark.

YOU WILL NEED
*Pencil*
*Ruler*
*Stiff card*
*Scissors*
*Assorted acrylic paints*
*Small paintbrush*

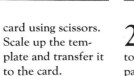 **1** Cut out a rectangle about 6 cm × 14 cm (2¼ in × 5½ in) in stiff card using scissors. Scale up the template and transfer it to the card.

**2** Draw in the detail and start to paint with acrylic paint, having mixed the colours to a creamy consistency. Allow to dry.

**3** Cut out the shape. Cut into the arms, leaving two slits to slot over a page of a book to mark your place.

# FLOWER COLLAGE

A collage is a good way of using up all sorts of scrap paper. Before you start, choose a theme. The subject here is a vase of flowers. Scissors are used to make the sharp edges, contrasting with pieces of torn paper for a varied effect. Sugar paper has a nice rough quality and can be easily torn into different shapes.

## YOU WILL NEED
*Scissors*
*Coloured paper*
*Strong clear glue*
*White card*

**1** Using scissors, cut up coloured paper for all the sharp edges such as the table top and vase. Tear lots of paper into plant-like shapes such as leaves and flowers.

**2** Place the pieces representing the table top and vase onto a large sheet of paper. Then stick them down in sequence with glue.

**3** Arrange the flowers and leaves and stick down the shapes with glue. Work in a systematic way, overlapping the shapes. When the design has dried, mount it onto a piece of white card to strengthen the completed collage.

# FINGER PUPPETS

This is a fun way to entertain yourself and the children without too much exertion. Have a great time creating the finger puppets and making up a play introducing all your own characters.

## YOU WILL NEED

*Thin white card*
*Scissors*
*Strong clear glue*
*Coloured gummed paper strips*
*Crêpe paper*
*Coloured tissue paper*
*Black and red felt-tip pens*

**1** Cut out a small rectangular piece of card, wrap it around your finger for size and trim it with scissors, allowing for a slight overlap. Stick down with glue to form a small tube, and hold until stuck.

**2** Cut strips of gummed paper to size with scissors. Moisten the back of the gummed paper with water and stick halfway down the small tube to represent clothes.

**3** Cut out a narrow strip of card 6 cm (2¼ in) long for the arms and cover with a narrow strip of coloured gummed paper, leaving a little piece of white card showing at both ends for the hands. Curve the centre of the strip around the body, making sure that an equal length of arm is visible either side of the tube. Glue in place halfway down.

**4** For added decoration, fringe a narrow strip of crêpe paper with scissors and stick onto the top edge of the gummed paper with glue.

**5** Finally, cut a narrow strip of coloured tissue paper for the hair and fringe with scissors. Then stick in onto the top end of the tube with glue. Draw a face and hands onto the areas which are left white with a black felt-tip pen. Fill in the lips and colour the cheeks with a red felt-tip pen.

# STAINED GLASS PICTURE

If you have ever admired stained glass in a church window, and wanted to make some for your own home, here is a simple method using tissue paper instead of glass, and black cartridge paper to emulate leading. You might like to suggest the name of your house in the design, and hang the picture in your front porch, or perhaps make some pretty decorative panels for a guest room or the arrival of a friend.

## YOU WILL NEED
*Pencil*
*Plain paper*
*Black paper*
*White pencil*
*Craft knife*
*Coloured tissue paper*
*Paper glue*
*Scissors*

**1** Design your stained glass picture on some plain paper, and then copy it onto a sheet of black paper with a white pencil. Using a craft knife, cut out the paper inside the white pencil lines to leave a black 'skeleton' framework.

**2** Draw around the black framework onto another sheet of black cartridge paper and cut it out.

**3** Work out where to place each colour, and then trace off each section of window onto a suitably coloured piece of tissue paper. Cut out the tissue slightly larger for gluing, and stick it to the back of one framework.

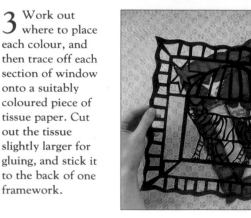

**4** Stick the second framework to the back of the first, pencil side in. When the frame has dried, suspend the picture in a strong light source to give the impression of stained glass.

# SILVER FRAME

This is an easy and cost-effective way of making a fancy frame without any special tools. All you need is some corrugated cardboard and silver baking foil.

## YOU WILL NEED
*Metal rule*
*Pencil*
*Craft knife*
*Heavy corrugated cardboard*
*Card*
*Paper glue*
*Silver baking foil*
*Scissors*
*Picture hanger*
*Masking tape*

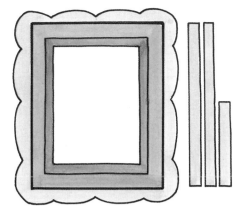

**1** Scale up the template to the size required. Using a craft knife and metal rule, cut out all the frame pieces from corrugated cardboard. Again using a craft knife and metal rule, cut out the spacers from card. Then glue together the two smaller borders of the frame.

**2** Glue the three spacers onto the underneath of the front frame. Stick the spacers onto the sides and bottom so that a gap is left at the top to insert a photograph.

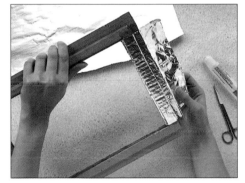

**3** Cover the border of the corrugated cardboard with foil. Trim it to size using scissors and glue down. Cover the back piece with foil.

**4** Using the point from a pair of scissors, pierce the back piece of the frame at the top, beneath the front border. Insert a picture hanger from the back. Cover the front of the hanger with masking tape.

**5** Finally spread glue onto the spacers and stick the front piece of the frame to the back.

# PAPER QUILLS

The old-fashioned paper craft known as quilling is used to make this distinctive card. You can design a picture in the same way, and hang it on the wall.

## YOU WILL NEED
Assorted coloured papers
Scissors
Strong clear glue
Contrasting coloured card

**1** Cut long narrow strips of various shades of coloured paper. First curl one end of each strip with the blunt edge of a pair of scissors, then, starting at this end, roll the strip into a tight coil.

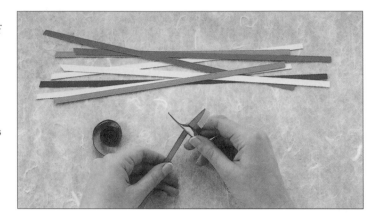

**2** Release the coil slightly and glue the end. Hold this in position until the glue is dry. Pinch the outside of the coils between your fingers to form different shapes such as a pear, scroll or eye.

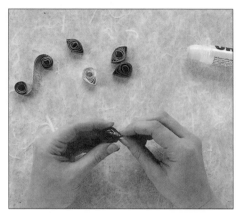

**3** Fold a rectangular piece of card in a contrasting colour in half. Arrange the shaped quills on the card and stick down, spreading the glue on the bottom edge of each quill.

# KITCHEN TOOL HOLDER

Turn an empty can into a decorative holder for kitchen tools. Try to find paper that emphasizes some detail in the kitchen, or even paint your own design on plain paper.

## YOU WILL NEED
*Empty can*
*White matt emulsion paint*
*Large paintbrush*
*Ruler*
*Pencil*
*Wrapping paper*
*Scissors*
*Strong clear glue*
*Clear polyurethane varnish*

**1** Prime the can with white matt emulsion paint. Measure the height and circumference of the can and draw two rectangles on the back of the wrapping paper slightly larger than these measurements, one for the inside of the can and one for the outside. Cut out the pieces. Spread glue on the piece for the inside.

**2** Insert this piece inside the can carefully and press it against the walls. Make cuts in the paper projecting at the top of the can so that the paper can be glued down neatly to the outside of the can.

**3** Glue the second piece of paper to the outside of the can, making sure the top edge is flush with the rim, and that there is a small overlap at the base. Cut the projecting paper so it can be glued to the bottom.

**4** Cut out a circle in the paper, using the can as a guide, and glue this to the base.

**5** Cut out a slightly smaller circle in the paper, glue it and lower it into the base of the can. Press into place. Allow to dry. Then apply two coats of clear polyurethane varnish. Allow to dry overnight.

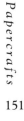

# RECYCLED BOX

This 'green' idea should appeal to everyone. Recycle clean old cardboard boxes which perhaps once contained tea bags and cover them with wrapping paper. They make attractive storage boxes for little bits and pieces such as necklaces or bracelets.

## YOU WILL NEED
*Cardboard box*
*Metal rule*
*Patterned and plain wrapping paper*
*Scissors*
*Paper glue*
*Coloured tissue paper*

**1** Measure all the sides of the box and cut patterned wrapping paper to the approximate size. Wrap the outside of the box with the paper, trim to size with scissors and stick it down with paper glue.

**2** Line the inside of the box with plain wrapping paper for neatness.

**3** Scrunch up some tissue paper that complements the colours of the wrapping paper and use to line the box.

# TISSUE BOX COVERS

This is a novel way to disguise tissue boxes and hide the brand names. Choose a wrapping paper that blends neatly into your colour scheme.

## YOU WILL NEED
*Tissue box*
*Metal rule*
*Thin white card*
*Pencil*
*Craft knife*
*Clear glue*
*Wrapping paper*
*Scissors*

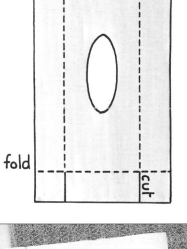

fold

cut

**1** Scale up the template to the size required to fit the tissue box, adding 12 mm (½ in) to all the measurements of the original tissue box. Transfer the pattern onto thin white card. Using a craft knife, cut out the pattern. Using a metal rule and craft knife lightly score all the edges that need to be folded. Be careful not to cut right through the card.

**2** Fold the top edges and the tabs, and stick the corners together with glue.

**3** Using the same template cut out the wrapping paper. Leave an overlap for the hole in the middle. Fold the paper under and cut darts in the paper. Glue underneath.

**4** Next stick the wrapping paper onto the white card with clear glue. Slip the cover over the tissue box and pull the tissues through the opening.

# GIFT-WRAPPED

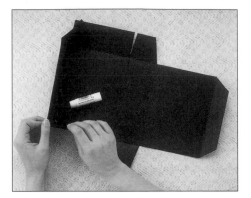

Add to the excitement of a special gift by packing it in this effective box. You can make the box any size, scaling the template up or down to fit the contents. Choose card and ribbon in colours to match your gift, if you like. The 'gems' can be bought from most craft suppliers.

## YOU WILL NEED
*Ruler*
*Pencil*
*Square of stiff card*
*Craft knife*
*Paper glue*
*Ribbon*
*Stapler*
*Jewel decorations*

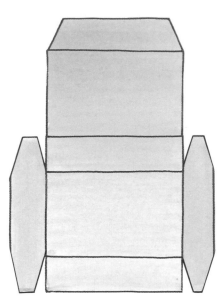

**1** Scale up the template to the size required and transfer the measurements onto the card. Cut out the box using a craft knife and ruler. Score along the inside fold of the tabs. Fold the card inwards to make a box. Glue down the tabs onto the inside of the box.

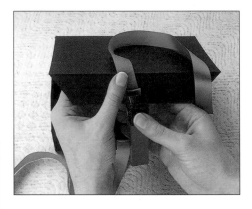

**2** Staple one piece of ribbon under the front flap of the box and fold the other piece under the staple onto the front flap of the lid in such a way that the staple does not show when the ribbon is tied.

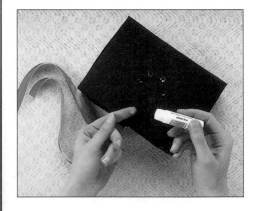

**3** Arrange the 'gems' on the lid in a pretty pattern and glue down. Tie the ribbon in a bow to finish and to hold the box shut.

# POP-UP
# CARD

This jolly cat pops out of a flowery garden and languidly surveys the scene. Use this simple design to make a variety of pop-up cards for different occasions.

## YOU WILL NEED
*Tracing paper*
*Pencil*
*Assortment of coloured cartridge papers*
*Scissors*
*Black paint*
*Small paintbrush*
*Ruler*
*Paper glue*

**1** Scale up the cat and flower templates. Draw in base tabs. Trace them onto coloured papers and cut out.

**2** Paint the details of the cut-outs in black.

**3** Cut a piece of paper 25 cm × 15 cm (10 in × 6 in). Fold it in half to form the base of the card. Measure a point 2.5 cm (1 in) from the top of the paper on the folded edge. Measure another point 4 cm (1½ in) from the folded edge along the top of the card. Draw a diagonal line between these two points. Make a fold inwards along this line, and open out the paper.

**4** Fold the cat cut-out in half, and then open it out. Glue the base tabs, and stick the cat along the diagonal lines on the inside of the card.

**5** Stick the flowers in position on the inside left of the card.

# CHRISTMAS CARD

Black card makes a dramatic background for the angel on this stylish handmade Christmas greeting. Try making a series of different designs on a similar theme.

### YOU WILL NEED
*Stiff card*
*Scissors*
*Image from old card or wrapping*
  *paper*
*Paper glue*
*Silver glitter pen*
*Gold self-adhesive stars*

**1** Cut the card to the size you require and fold it in half. Score along the inside of the fold to make a sharp, neat edge. Cut out an image and glue onto the centre of the card.

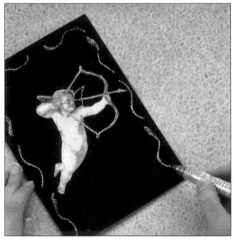

**2** Draw some elegant lines with a silver glitter pen around the edge of the card, and allow to dry.

**3** Arrange a cluster of gold stars around the central image and a line of them spaced evenly on top of the silver lines to create a border.

# DECORATING PAPER

It is fun to design your own wrapping paper. This rustic paper with its oak leaf motif could be used to wrap a woolly sweater in earthy colours, or perhaps some gardening tools. You could even print a friend's name with rubber stamps in the form of letters, or perhaps your own special message.

## YOU WILL NEED
*Pencil*
*Erasers*
*Craft knife*
*Assorted poster paints, or ink pads*
*Small paintbrush*
*Assorted wrapping papers*

**1** Draw a simple design onto an eraser and cut around it with a craft knife, taking great care to avoid your fingers.

**2** Apply a coat of paint to the image on your rubber stamp, and press the stamp down firmly onto the wrapping paper. Take care not to make the paint too runny, as it would spread and blur the image. Alternatively, press the stamp onto an ink pad.

**3** A more delicate effect is achieved by printing on white tissue paper, which would be particularly suitable for wrapping wedding or christening gifts.

# GIFT TAGS

Why buy expensive gift tags when you can make your own from scraps of paper? Match or contrast the tags with the wrapping paper, or make plain ones and decorate them with sequins, scraps of felt, coloured foil or glitter.

## YOU WILL NEED
*Ruler*
*Scraps of coloured paper*
*Scissors*
*Pencil*
*Paper glue*
*Hole punch*
*Thin string*

**1** Cut a 10 cm × 5 cm (4 in × 2 in) piece of coloured paper. Fold it in half.

**2** Draw hearts and wavy lines onto contrasting pieces of coloured paper and cut them out.

**3** Stick them in place with paper glue.

**4** Punch a hole on the inside top left-hand corner of the gift tag. Thread a length of thin string through the hole.

# STATIONERY SET

Co-ordinated stationery looks very attractive — you might like to make a complete set for all your correspondence, including invitation cards. You could choose a simple motif such as a star or heart, or perhaps your initials or a monogram. You could also make this stationery wallet to keep everything together.

## YOU WILL NEED
*Pencil*
*Scraps of paper in contrasting colours*
*Sheets of writing paper and envelopes*
*Scissors*
*Paper glue*
*Piece of thin card in complementary*
*    colour*

**1** Draw your design onto paper that contrasts with or complements the colour of your writing paper. Cut out each element of the design.

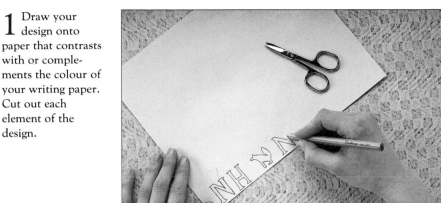

**2** Place the cut-outs on the stationery and stick in position. You might prefer the top left-hand corner, or perhaps the top centre of each sheet of paper. The back or front of each envelope may be decorated similarly.

**3** Cut out a stationery wallet in thin card to hold the paper. The wallet may be decorated in the same way as the stationery.

# PLACE CARDS

Place cards can set the mood for a meal. Perhaps you want to convey a sophisticated atmosphere with very plain cards, or a jazzy, fun air with bright, vivid colours and clever cut-outs. You can also follow the theme of the occasion such as a birthday or anniversary celebration.

### YOU WILL NEED
*Paper in a variety of colours*
*Scraps of paper in contrasting colours*
*Pencil*
*Scissors*
*Paper glue*
*Black felt-tip pen*

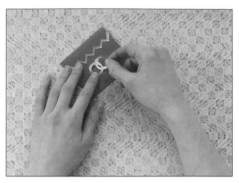

**1** Cut a small rectangle of cartridge paper. Draw your chosen design onto contrasting paper and cut it out.

**2** Fold a small piece of coloured paper in half to form the place card. Position each element of the design, and stick it in place.

**3** Write the name of a guest on each place card.

# CHRISTMAS CRACKER

Decorate your Christmas tree with lots of fancy crackers. Fill them with tiny gifts and pull them during the festive season.

## YOU WILL NEED
*Cardboard tube*
*Silver doily*
*Scissors*
*Crêpe paper*
*Strong clear glue*
*Ribbon*
*Foil ribbon*

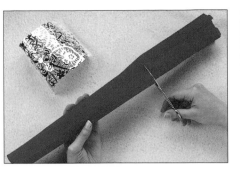

**1** Place the cardboard tube on top of the silver doily and trim the doily to size using scissors.

**2** Place the cardboard tube on a length of crêpe paper which will cover the whole tube. Trim the ends, leaving at least 10 cm (4 in) at both ends. Glue the crêpe paper where the seam is formed. Next place the silver doily on top of the tube and glue down.

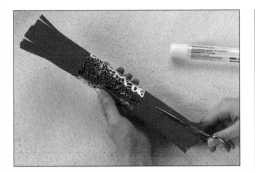

**3** When this is secure, fringe the ends of the crêpe paper. This is done by cutting into the ends with scissors at regular intervals all around the circumference.

**4** Next cut two lengths of ribbon about 30 cm (12 in) long and tie a bow at both ends of the cracker.

**5** Pull long strips of the foil ribbon through closed scissors to make it twist and curl into ringlets. Tie onto both ends of the cracker.

# FLOWER GARLAND

Festoon a ceiling and walls with festive flower garlands made of coloured tissue paper. Use bright colours for the flowers, and green for the leaves.

## YOU WILL NEED
*Coloured tissue paper*
*Thin card*
*Black felt-tip pen*
*Scissors*
*Paper glue*
*Coloured string*

**3** Fold the shapes in half so that you can cut a hole neatly in the centre, using the scissors.

**4** For each flower, glue the centre of a brightly coloured shape and place directly on top of another shape of the same coloured tissue paper. Press down firmly.

**1** Fold sheets of tissue paper so that a number of shapes can be cut simultaneously. Scale up the flower shape on the template onto card and draw around it with a black pen onto the folded sheets of tissue.

**2** Cut out the flower shape with scissors, keeping the layers together. Repeat this until you have enough shapes of different colours.

**5** The leaves are formed in the same way as the flowers, by gluing in the centre. To join the flowers and leaves, glue the tips of three petals on one side of a flower shape and place a green shape on top. Continue sticking the shapes alternately at the tips and centre. Alternate leaves and flowers until the garland is built up.

**6** Finally, thread a piece of coloured string through the central holes to hang the garland.

# LAMPSHADE

Dress up that jaded shade by covering it with wrapping paper or wallpaper. The design or colours of the shade can be chosen to co-ordinate with the furnishing scheme of your room.

## YOU WILL NEED
*Lampshade*
*Brown parcel paper*
*Wrapping paper or wallpaper*
*Pencil*
*Craft knife*
*Coin*
*Scissors*
*Clear glue*
*Masking tape*
*Clear polyurethane varnish*
*Large paintbrush*

**1** Lay the lampshade on its side on the brown parcel paper and slowly rotate it, drawing the shape as you go along to achieve the correct measurement. Use this shape as the template for the lampshade.

**2** Cut out the brown parcel paper shape slightly outside the drawn line using a craft knife. Draw a scalloped edge using a coin as a template and cut out scallops.

**3** Place the template onto the wrong side of the wrapping paper and secure with masking tape. Then draw around the template and cut out this shape.

**4** Spread glue onto the lampshade and stick down the paper slowly, smoothing out any bumps or air pockets as you go round.

**5** Make cuts in the protruding paper at the top so that it can be glued down neatly to the inside of the frame. Apply two coats of clear polyurethane varnish so that the lampshade may be wiped clean.

### Decorating objects

Decoupage is a way of decorating almost any object or surface with cut-out pieces of paper to achieve a pictorial or abstract design. You can decorate cardboard boxes, metal objects such as old buckets and cake tins, glass or ceramic vases and wooden items such as jewellery boxes and caskets. The materials and equipment you will need for decoupage are inexpensive and easy to obtain from arts and crafts shops. After the paper pieces are applied, the design is sealed and protected with several coats of varnish. Decoupage can also be used over larger areas to decorate furniture, doors and even walls.

### Choosing materials

Decorative images for decoupage are all around you in the form of magazines, old greetings cards, wrapping paper, picture postcards, illustrated catalogues and paper packaging. Photocopies work well too – colour ones just need cutting out and applying, while black and white copies can be hand-coloured or used as they are to create striking monochrome designs. Tissue paper, coloured and hand-made paper give interesting effects – tissue paper can look almost translucent when given several coats of varnish.

### Preparing surfaces

Surfaces for decoupage need to be clean, dry and smooth. Clean old metal objects with heavy-duty wire (steel) wool, then rinse in a solution of one part water to one part vinegar. Use the same solution to rinse new metal. Metal objects may also need two coats of rust-resistant paint. Wooden surfaces should be lightly sanded, then wiped with white spirit. Seal porous surfaces with matt emulsion paint (*above*); wipe down glass and ceramic surfaces to remove grease and dust.

### Cutting out

At times it may be easier to cut out shapes roughly using large scissors and leave a generous margin round the image. Change to small scissors to cut out the details (*below*). You may prefer to use a craft knife and cutting mat for intricate designs.

## Sticking the shapes in position

Use PVA glue at full strength for sticking down shapes (*right*). Tweezers are useful for picking up and positioning small, delicate cut-out shapes while scissors are useful when handling larger pieces. Check that all the shapes are stuck down well before varnishing and add extra glue where necessary. When the pieces have been stuck down, cover with a slightly damp cloth and press with a roller to remove air bubbles.

## Varnishing

Make sure the decoupage is thoroughly dry before varnishing. You can use anything between two and 20 coats of varnish, allowing each layer to dry in a dust-free place. The more coats of varnish you apply, the smoother the surface of the finished object will feel to the touch. Between coats, sand the surface lightly, then wipe with a damp cloth.

When varnishing, use a household paintbrush (kept specially for varnish) and apply the varnish with smooth, even strokes in one direction, avoiding drips. You may want to wipe off a stained varnish as you work to achieve a coloured effect (*below*).

Use PVA glue diluted two parts water to one part PVA or a clear polyurethane wood varnish (choose a non-toxic type). Artists' acrylic varnish is more expensive, but it will not yellow with age. Varnishes containing coloured stains can be used to make a piece of decoupage look old. A decorative effect can be achieved with crackle varnish, or two varnishes used together to create a decoratively cracked and crazed surface, colouring the cracks with artists' oil paints.

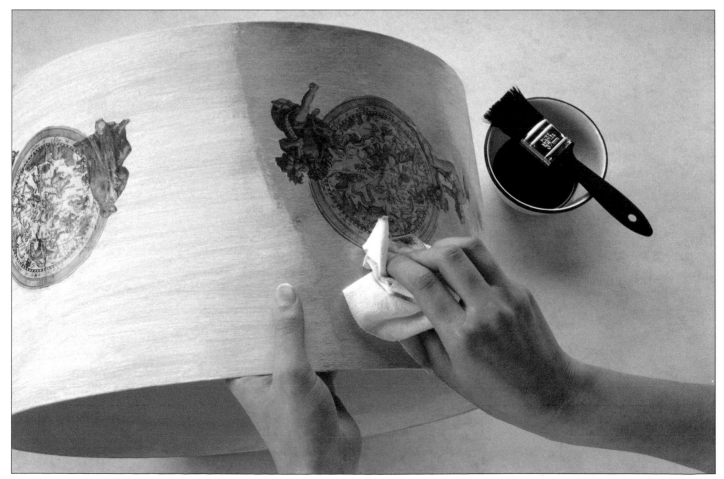

# GIFT BOXES

Presents always seem more intriguing if packed in a special box — here are two that have been decorated with holly leaves for Christmas and flowers for spring. Other suitable motifs include Christmas trees, angels and reindeer.

**1** Using a pencil, draw your designs onto coloured paper.

## YOU WILL NEED
*Assortment of coloured paper or old*
    *catalogues*
*Pencil*
*Scissors*
*Gift boxes*
*Paper glue*

**2** Cut them out carefully using scissors.

**3** Arrange the cut-outs on the gift box and stick them in position with paper glue.

**4** As an alternative, cover a plain gold gift box with photographs of flowers cut out of a seed catalogue.

# MODEL CLOCK

This highly original timepiece would delight any collector of bizarre objects! The figure is typical of the models daringly featured in Victorian mail-order catalogues.

## YOU WILL NEED
*Drill*
*Piece of plywood*
*Paper images from old magazines*
*Scissors*
*Diluted PVA glue*
*Pencil*
*Dark oak-coloured varnish*
*Small paintbrush*
*Soft cloth*
*Clear matt varnish*
*Clock mechanism*
*Clock hands*
*Battery*

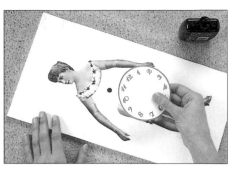

**1** Drill a hole, large enough for a clock mechanism, in a primed piece of plywood. Cut out suitable paper images and clock face and arrange on the piece of plywood.

**2** Make sure that the centre of the clock face is directly above the drilled hole. Stick the design in position using diluted PVA glue. Rub the paper with your hands until it is smooth. Using a pencil, pierce a hole in the centre of the clock face.

**3** Allow 1 hour for the glue to dry, then apply dark oak-coloured varnish with a small paintbrush. Before it dries, rub it off in circular movements with a soft cloth, working from the centre outwards. Leave to dry.

**4** Apply a coat of clear matt varnish. When this is dry, fit the clock mechanism and connect the hands to the front. Insert the battery.

# WASTE PAPER BASKET

Decoupage decoration quickly covers surfaces in beautiful and unusual designs. It is particularly effective on shiny materials, such as this metal waste paper basket.

## YOU WILL NEED
*Flat brush*
*Diluted PVA glue*
*Metal waste paper basket*
*Pale blue and yellow tissue paper*
*Scissors*
*Flowery wrapping paper*
*Clear polyurethane varnish*

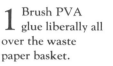

**1** Brush PVA glue liberally all over the waste paper basket.

**2** Tear long strips of tissue paper and paste them round the middle area of the basket.

**3** Cut out an assortment of strips and pretty motifs from wrapping paper.

**4** Decide on the design of the basket and dip the pieces of wrapping paper in PVA glue. Stick them onto the basket according to your chosen design, brushing them flat as you work. Add more strips of tissue paper until the design is complete. Leave to dry. Finish with a final coat of glue and leave to dry. Cover with a coat of clear polyurethane varnish and leave to dry.

# HAT BOX

This traditional hat box can be used to store a variety of objects other than hats. It is also an attractive piece to display in your home. A simple form of decoupage using wrapping paper is shown here. You can of course cut out pictures from magazines, old postcards and greeting cards, building up layers of images.

## YOU WILL NEED
*Hat box*
*White matt emulsion paint*
*Large paintbrush*
*Fine sandpaper*
*Piece of natural sponge*
*Poster paint*
*Rag*
*Wrapping paper*
*Scissors*
*Diluted PVA glue*
*Coloured varnish*

**1** Paint the hat box with matt white emulsion paint. Rub down using fine sandpaper. Using a piece of natural sponge, add a wash of watery paint to age the box, removing some of the paint with a rag as you go.

**2** Choose a paper with an attractive design and cut out the images that most appeal to you. Arrange the paper on the box ready to glue on.

**3** Glue your images onto the box using diluted PVA glue and leave to dry.

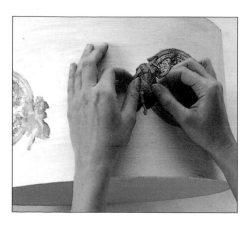

**4** Varnish the box with a coloured varnish, again removing a lot of it with a rag to give the box warmth and to add to its antiqued look.

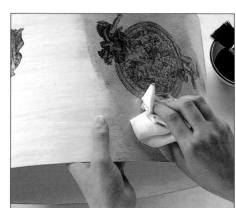

# SHOE BOX

The pictures of shoes decorating this box have been dipped in cold tea to antique them. This technique is very effective, and a variety of different images could be used. For example, pictures of hats could adorn a circular hat box, or jewels a trinket box. Good sources of illustrations are old clothing catalogues, greetings cards, and any Victorian or Edwardian technical manuals.

## YOU WILL NEED
*Brown wrapping paper*
*Cardboard shoe box*
*Scissors*
*Paper glue*
*Old shoe catalogues*
*Cold tea*

**1** Cut out pieces of brown wrapping paper to fit a cardboard shoe box. Use to cover the box and lid completely and glue in place.

**2** Roughly cut out the chosen images from the catalogues. Fill a small bowl with cold tea, and submerge each image for a few seconds so that the tea penetrates the paper. Pin each image up to dry. If the images hang vertically, this should prevent them from wrinkling as they dry. If they do become a little creased, press them quickly on the reverse using a cool iron.

**3** Cut around the pictures carefully with small scissors and arrange them on the box and lid.

**4** When you are satisfied with your design, stick each picture in position.

# HAND MIRROR

Decorate a dull hand mirror with ornate decoupage motifs to add a beautiful touch to the dressing table. You could even make a matching set with a decorated hairbrush and other toilet items.

## YOU WILL NEED
*Plastic hand mirror*
*Fine sandpaper*
*Plain paper*
*Masking tape*
*Scissors*
*Poster paint in a complementary colour*
*Small paintbrush*
*Wrapping paper*
*Diluted PVA glue*

**1** Lightly sand the plain surfaces of the mirror using fine sandpaper.

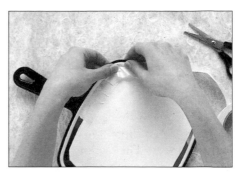

**2** Cut out a plain paper shield to fit over the mirror glass and stick in place with masking tape.

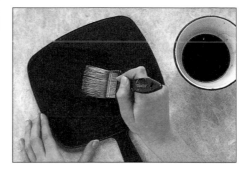

**3** Paint the plastic surfaces with poster paint, allowing each coat to dry thoroughly.

**4** Cut out motifs from wrapping paper and arrange over the handle and back of the mirror. Dip each piece into diluted PVA, place on the mirror and brush more glue on top.

**5** Using small strips of wrapping paper, decorate the rim and front edge in the same way. Leave to dry overnight. Remove the paper and tape from the front edge.

# CAKE TIN

This metal cake tin has been given a new lease of life with some white paint and jazzy tartlet motifs — you could, of course, depict any type of confectionery you wanted!

## YOU WILL NEED
*Metal cake tin*
*White poster paint*
*Paintbrush*
*Pencil*
*Coloured cartridge paper*
*Scissors*
*Paper glue*
*Clear gloss varnish*

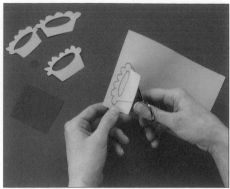

**1** Wash the cake tin to remove any grease and then prime the outside with a coat of white paint. Leave to dry, then apply a second coat to give a good dense base colour.

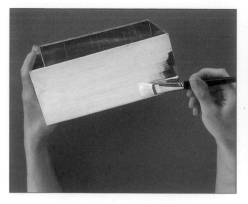

**2** Draw your designs onto cartridge paper and cut them out.

**3** Arrange the cutouts on the sides and lid of the tin. Stick them in position with glue.

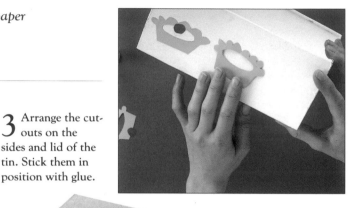

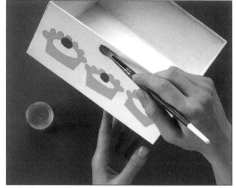

**4** Seal the tin with two coats of varnish. Allow to dry thoroughly before you use the tin.

# PRIVATE
# LETTER BOX

This ornate box can be used to store those secret letters, or to keep documents safe. Use brightly coloured wrapping paper to decorate it, saving oddments for extra details.

## YOU WILL NEED
*Thin cardboard*
*Scissors*
*Craft knife*
*Metal rule*
*Strong clear glue*
*Masking tape*
*Wrapping paper*
*Large paintbrush*
*Diluted PVA glue*
*Narrow ribbon*
*Button*

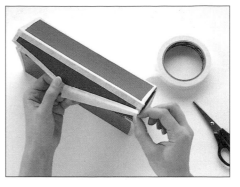

**2** Strengthen the edges of the box with strips of masking tape.

**1** Scale up the template to the size required and transfer to a piece of thin cardboard. Cut out the box shape. Score along the folds using a craft knife and metal rule. Fold in the tabs and glue firmly in place along the sides.

**3** Cut out motifs from wrapping paper and decide where to position them on the box. Stick down with diluted PVA glue, brushing an extra coat of glue over the pieces to varnish them. Allow to dry. Fix a loop of ribbon under the flap of the lid and a button on the front of the box to fasten.

# CUPID CUPBOARD

If you see a shabby old cupboard in an auction sale, why not bid for it? Decoupage is an easy way to turn such a piece of furniture into a charming addition to your home, and you do not need to have any special artistic skills.

## YOU WILL NEED
*Scissors*
*Decorative paper images*
*Small cupboard*
*Medium sandpaper*
*White spirit*
*White matt emulsion paint*
*Diluted wood glue*
*Small paintbrush*
*Acrylic varnish*
*Large paintbrush*
*Antique oak-coloured varnish*
*Soft cloth*

**1** Using scissors, cut out the decorative images required for the decoupage.

**2** To prepare the cupboard, rub down with sandpaper, clean with white spirit and coat twice with white matt emulsion paint. Arrange the cut-out images on the cupboard and stick down with diluted wood glue. Make sure the glue is spread evenly over the images. Leave to dry for 1 hour.

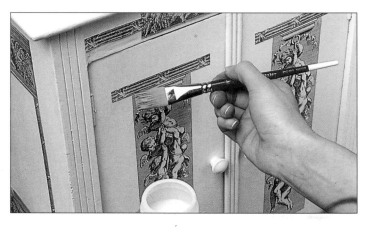

**3** Using a small paintbrush, apply a coat of acrylic varnish to the decoupage images only. This will protect them against the next stage of varnishing. Allow the acrylic varnish to dry for 30 minutes.

**4** Using a large paintbrush, apply the antique oak-coloured varnish to small areas at a time. As soon as you have brushed on the varnish, wipe it off quickly with a soft cloth. Repeat this process until the whole cupboard has been varnished. This stains the white painted areas while the oak-coloured varnish stays intact in cracks and grooves.

# MOSAIC TRAY

Create a useful and evocative souvenir of your travels with a collection of postcards. Select a variety of pictures that capture your memories, or those of a friend or relative, and use to transform an old tray into a piece of art.

## YOU WILL NEED
*Old tray*
*Sandpaper*
*White matt emulsion paint*
*PVA glue*
*Blue poster paint*
*Large paintbrush*
*Scissors*
*Assorted picture postcards*

**1** Clean and lightly sand the tray. Prime with one coat of white emulsion. Leave to dry. Mix two tablespoons of PVA glue with the blue poster paint and apply one coat to the tray. Leave to dry. Cut up picture postcards into triangles.

**2** Decide on the arrangement of the images on the tray. Mix ¾ cup PVA to ¼ cup water. Dip each triangle into the glue and position on the tray, turning the tray as you work. Add small strips cut from postcards along the top edges of the tray. When the design is complete, varnish the tray with two coats of PVA glue.

# DECORATING FURNITURE TECHNIQUES

### Decorating furniture

It is quite easy to transform an old but sound piece of furniture and give it a new lease of life by using a simple decorative technique. You will need no special artistic skills, but time spent preparing the surface will enhance the finished result.

### Preparation

Both old and new wood should be specially prepared before decoration. Remove existing wax, paint and varnish from old pieces with a liquid paint stripper, available in paint and hardware stores. You may need to apply several coats of stripper before you get down to the bare wood. After stripping, rub the surfaces down with fine sandpaper (*above*), then wipe down with a lint-free rag dipped in white spirit.

Fill scars and dents with an all-purpose wood filler and sand smooth when dry. Remove any rough patches from new wood by sanding, then wipe down with a damp cloth or white spirit as before. Prime the wood before decorating by applying one or two coats of white matt emulsion (*left*).

Sandpaper comes in a range of textures, but you should choose medium grade for sanding down bare wood and filled patches. Use fine grade for rubbing down between coats of paint or varnish. Wire (steel) wool can be used instead of sandpaper and it is much more manoeuvrable on rounded surfaces or mouldings than sandpaper which is rather stiff. When sanding, always follow the grain of the wood. For flat surfaces, wrap your sheet of sandpaper round a small block of wood or cork for easier handling.

## Decorative techniques

There are many techniques you can use to decorate a piece of furniture. Sponging and stippling create interesting surface textures and look very attractive when subtle colour schemes are used. Pictorial and abstract patterns can be stencilled or painted freehand on the piece (*right*). Wax can be used to distress and age the surface of a piece of furniture painted with two coats of paint, so the base colour shows through as though the top colour has been worn away with time.

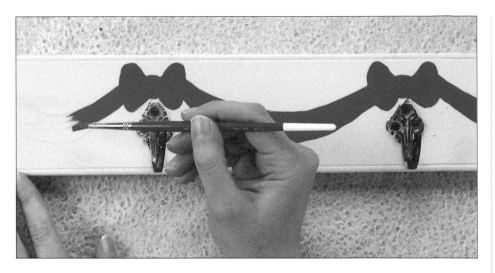

## Paint and stains

Matt, water-based paints are the best choice for decorating furniture. They can be thinned with water to the desired consistency and brushes are easy to clean with warm, soapy water. Allow each coat of paint to dry thoroughly before applying the next as damp paint may wrinkle or bubble under a new layer. Water-soluble stains can be applied to bare wood with a brush or a soft cloth to form the background to your design instead of the usual matt emulsion.

## Brushes

For priming, painting large areas and varnishing, use good-quality household paintbrushes with a natural bristle filling. For most projects, choose either a 2.5, 4 or 5 cm (1, 1½ or 2 in) brush. Take care to clean brushes thoroughly after use and store them standing on their handles in a clean container, or hang them up in a dry shed or garage. Use artists' paintbrushes for accuracy when painting details and intricate designs – natural sable is considered the best filling, but this is expensive so you may prefer to buy one or two brushes with synthetic bristles.

## Finishing off

After you have finished decorating your piece of furniture, seal and protect the design from chipping and general wear and tear with two or more coats of varnish (*below*).

You can buy varnish in several different finishes – matt, satin or gloss – and the choice is really up to you. Matt varnish gives a soft, flat finish; satin has a slight sheen and gloss has a deep shine. You will need to apply at least two coats and rub the surface down lightly with fine grade wire (steel) wool between coats. Allow each coat to dry thoroughly before rubbing down. Use a standard household paintbrush to apply the varnish and cover the furniture with smooth, even strokes around edges and mouldings.

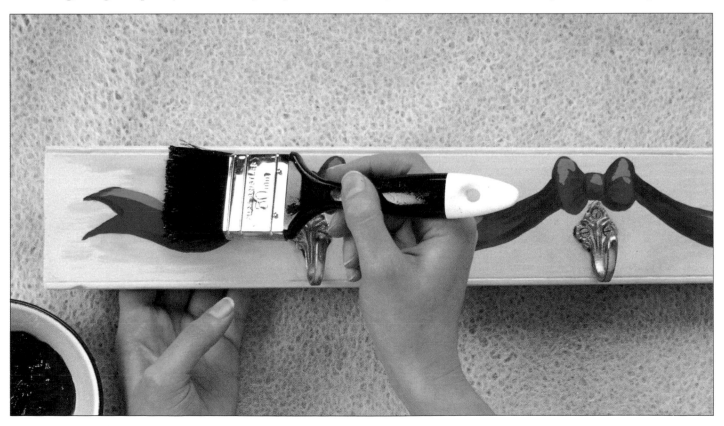

# I V Y
# M I R R O R

'Mirror, mirror on the wall — who is the fairest of them all?' By painting a trail of ivy on the frame, this mirror becomes a decorative feature for a country bedroom. Experiment using alternative designs made up of flowers or intricately-shaped leaves.

## YOU WILL NEED
*Wooden-framed mirror*
*Masking tape*
*White matt emulsion paint*
*Large paintbrush*
*Paper*
*Pencil*
*Carbon paper*
*Small paintbrush*
*Green and white acrylic paint*
*Soft cloths*
*Finishing wax*

**1** Prepare the mirror. Put strips of masking tape all round the edges of the mirror close to the frame to prevent paint from getting onto the mirror. Apply two coats of white matt emulsion paint.

**2** Draw an ivy design onto paper to fit the mirror. Place a strip of carbon paper face down on the mirror frame and secure with masking tape. Lay the ivy design on top and secure in the same way. Draw around the design with a pencil so it is reproduced on the frame in carbon. Repeat this process until the whole design is copied onto the frame.

**3** Using a small paintbrush, paint the meander-ing ivy with a mixture of green and white acrylic paint.

**4** Use a darker mixture of green to paint an outline and other details. Using a soft cloth, polish the mirror frame with two coats of finishing wax. Allow each coat to dry and polish again.

**5** When the wax is dry, remove the masking tape to reveal a clean mirror.

# PAINTED BUCKET

This bucket is influenced by the canal boat painters and uses their traditional colours of green, red and yellow.

## YOU WILL NEED
Metal bucket
Wire (steel) wool
Green, red, yellow and black enamel paint
Large paintbrush
Pencil
Tracing paper
White paper
Chalk
Masking tape
Small paintbrush

**1** Rub down the bucket with wire wool. Paint it with two coats of green enamel paint using a large paintbrush. Scale up the template to fit your bucket, tracing the design onto paper. Rub chalk onto the back of the template and attach to the bucket side with masking tape. Draw the design on top with a pencil and the image will be duplicated in chalk.

**2** Remove the template carefully so as not to disturb the chalk. Paint the areas of red and yellow using a small brush. Apply two coats and allow to dry for 6 hours between each coat.

**3** When all the colours are dry, finish off by adding black outlines and details with a small paintbrush. Allow the paint to dry forming a tough coat. Varnish is not necessary for this piece.

# TOY CHEST

This colourful chest can be used in a child's room for storing toys and puzzles. Try to think of as many different colours as you can for the kites and bows — experiment with mixing your own shades.

## YOU WILL NEED
*Toy chest*
*White matt emulsion paint*
*Large paintbrush*
*Sandpaper*
*White chalk*
*Stiff black card*
*Scissors*
*Pencil*
*Assorted acrylic paints*
*Small paintbrush*
*Masking tape*
*Clear satin polyurethane varnish*

**1** Prepare the chest. Paint it white, leave to dry and rub down with sandpaper. Apply a second coat of white paint and leave to dry. Scale up and draw the shape of the kite and bows with white chalk on black card and cut them out. Hold the templates against the chest and move them around until you have arranged them satisfactorily. Then draw around each template with a pencil. Draw in the detail and link up the bows and kites with a flowing pencil line.

**2** Using a small paintbrush, paint the edges of the chest in blue acrylic paint, covering the borders with masking tape to give a neat line.

**3** Start painting in the design. You may need to give it a couple of coats to achieve an even finish. Using a small paintbrush in a confident manner, link up the bows following your flowing pencil line with burnt umber acrylic paints. Add the finishing touches with a paler tone of each colour to add movement and dimension. Allow to dry. Apply polyurethane varnish, giving the chest at least two coats for maximum protection. Leave to dry overnight.

# FOOT STOOL

The red tulips and blue decoration on this stool are reminiscent of early American folk art. This idea can be adapted to transform any piece of secondhand furniture.

## YOU WILL NEED
Stool
Sandpaper
White matt emulsion paint
Metal rule
Plain paper
Pencil
Scissors
Coloured chalk
Masking tape
Soft cloth
Assorted gouache paints
Small paintbrush
Gloss polyurethane varnish

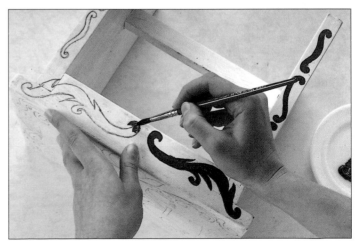

1 Rub down the stool with sandpaper and paint with matt white emulsion paint. Measure the surfaces to be decorated, then draw the planned design onto paper. Cut out to size. Completely cover the back of the paper with chalk. Hold it in place on the stool with masking tape. Draw over the design firmly with pencil, and remove the drawing paper. Follow the chalk design carefully and lightly with pencil, and wipe off the loose chalk with a soft cloth.

2 Paint on the design with gouache paints using a small paintbrush. Leave to dry. Then seal the stool with two coats of gloss polyurethane varnish.

# SIDE TABLE

You might find an old piece of furniture that has a pleasing shape or line but is in terrible condition. Strip off any old paint and start again. This is a very simple linear design painted on just such a 'rescued' table. Masking tape is invaluable for helping to paint straight lines.

## YOU WILL NEED
*Table*
*White matt emulsion paint*
*Large paintbrush*
*Yellow ochre and raw umber acrylic paints*
*Ruler*
*Pencil*
*Masking tape*
*Small paintbrush*
*Antique pine-coloured varnish*
*Soft cloth*
*Matt varnish*

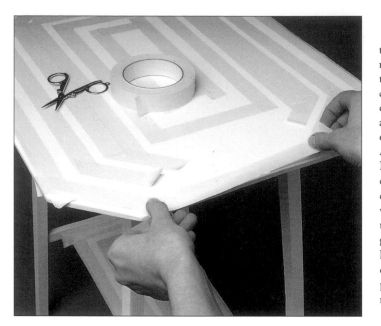

1 Prepare the table. Apply two coats of white matt emulsion. For the base cream colour, mix yellow ochre acrylic paint and white matt emulsion paint. Apply two coats. Measure and mark out the linear design on the table with a pencil. Using the markings as a guide, lay down long parallel strips of masking tape to protect the areas not to be painted.

2 Using a small paintbrush, fill in the exposed areas. This design starts with a dark tone which gets gradually lighter. To achieve this, mix raw umber acrylic paint and white matt emulsion paint in the required proportions. Allow to dry for 30 minutes.

3 When the paint is completely dry, peel off all the masking tape carefully. A little retouching may be needed at this point.

4 Next, brush on the antique pine-coloured varnish with a large paintbrush, working in small areas at a time, and rub it off immediately with a soft cloth. Repeat this until the whole table has been covered to give it a nice warm tone. Finally, give the table a coat of matt varnish with a large paintbrush, in a well-ventilated room.

# WICKER BASKET

Here an ordinary wicker basket is given a new lease of life for a baby's room. When choosing a basket, look out for little details which you can emphasize to give it that personal touch.

## YOU WILL NEED
*Wicker basket*
*White matt emulsion paint*
*Large paintbrush*
*Blue and red acrylic paint*
*Small paintbrush*

**1** First paint the inside and outside of the wicker basket with white matt emulsion paint, using a large paintbrush.

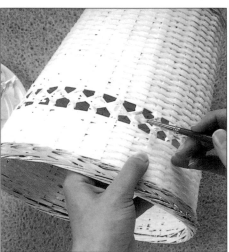

**2** When the white paint is dry, mix a little blue acrylic paint with some white matt emulsion paint to make a baby blue. Also mix a little red acrylic paint with some white matt emulsion to make a baby pink. Using a small paintbrush, pick out the detail on the wicker basket in contrasting colours.

# DESIGNER SHELVES

These pretty shelves are in the tradition of tole painting. You can make them to any size or renovate old or existing shelving. Choose colours to match the room; a combination of blue and white is both simple and effective. Practise the brush strokes on a piece of paper before you start, to gain enough confidence to achieve the design.

## YOU WILL NEED
*Shelves*
*White matt emulsion paint*
*Large paintbrush*
*Fine sandpaper*
*Pencil*
*Blue acrylic paint*
*Small paintbrush*
*Clear polyurethane varnish*

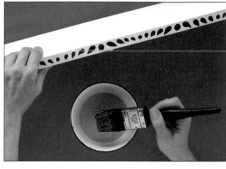

1 Prime the shelves with white emulsion paint and rub down with fine sandpaper. Pencil on the design.

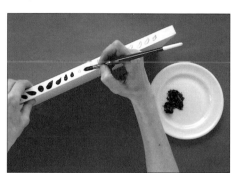

2 Mix the blue acrylic paint to a creamy consistency. Paint the design gently but precisely using single confident brush strokes.

3 Varnish the finished shelves with clear polyurethane varnish to protect the design and so that they may be wiped clean.

# HOOK BOARD

Brighten up your hallway by painting a simple bow motif to join coat hooks on an old length of board, and attach it to the wall.

## YOU WILL NEED
*Length of board with coat hooks*
*Medium sandpaper*
*White spirit*
*Soft cloth*
*White matt emulsion paint*
*Large paintbrush*
*Assorted acrylic paints*
*Pencil*
*Small paintbrush*
*Metallic gold paint*
*Clear gloss varnish*

**1** Sand the length of board until it is smooth. Then wipe the surface with white spirit and a soft cloth.

**2** Apply a coat of white matt emulsion paint with a large paintbrush. Leave for 30 minutes to dry.

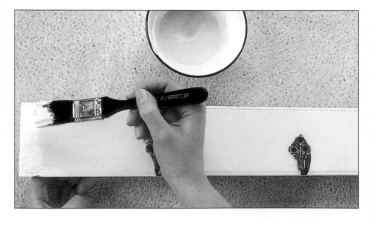

**3** Mix up a buttermilk colour with a little yellow ochre acrylic paint and some white matt emulsion paint. Apply two coats, avoiding the hooks.

**4** Then draw a bow motif onto the board using a pencil. Fill in the design with red acrylic paint using a small paintbrush. Leave for 10 minutes to dry.

**5** Using a small paintbrush, make little strokes to suggest highlights with a mixture of red acrylic and white matt emulsion paint, and shadows with a mixture of red and raw umber acrylic paint. Allow to dry.

**6** Then using a small paint-brush, paint the metal hooks with metallic gold paint.

**7** Finally, when all the paint is dry, apply a coat of clear gloss varnish, working in a well-ventilated room.

# KITCHEN CHAIR

Here the technique of distressing is used. The yellow underneath the top coat of paint shows through on the finished chair as if the colour had worn away with time. On this piece, less traditional colours have been used. The colours you use on your chair can of course complement those in your kitchen.

## YOU WILL NEED
*Kitchen chair*
*White matt emulsion paint*
*Yellow and blue vinyl matt emulsion paint*
*Large paintbrush*
*Soft cloth*
*Beeswax*
*Medium sandpaper*
*Pencil*
*White paper*
*White chalk*
*Masking tape*
*Small paintbrush*
*Diluted blue acrylic paint*

**1** Prepare the chair. Prime it with two coats of white matt emulsion paint, then apply two coats of yellow vinyl matt emulsion paint using a large paintbrush. Allow to dry for 2 hours.

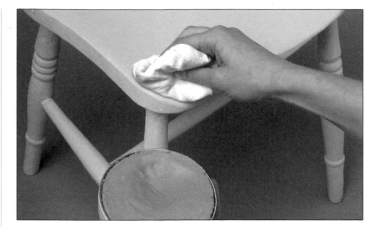

**2** Using a cloth, apply a liberal layer of beeswax on the areas where the chair would normally become worn, such as the edges and the seat. Leave to dry for 2 hours.

**3** Then apply one coat of blue vinyl matt emulsion paint with a large paintbrush. Leave for 1 hour or until the chair is completely dry.

**4** Next, using a piece of medium sandpaper, rub down the entire chair, concentrating particularly on the areas where the beeswax was applied. This will expose patches of the yellow under-coat. Remove all dust with a soft dry cloth before the next step.

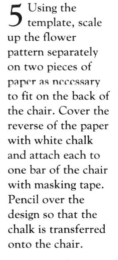

**5** Using the template, scale up the flower pattern separately on two pieces of paper as necessary to fit on the back of the chair. Cover the reverse of the paper with white chalk and attach each to one bar of the chair with masking tape. Pencil over the design so that the chalk is transferred onto the chair.

**6** Using a small paintbrush, fill in the areas of the design with diluted blue acrylic paint. The paint sits lightly on the wax and has a faint textured effect when dry.

**7** To finish off the piece and to protect it, apply two layers of beeswax, allowing 1 hour to dry between coats.

*Decorating Furniture*

# BEDSIDE CUPBOARD

A fleur-de-lys is always an elegant motif and looks most impressive gilded, as on this bedside cupboard.

## YOU WILL NEED
*Bedside cupboard*
*White matt emulsion paint*
*Large paintbrush*
*Paper*
*Pencil*
*Green acrylic paint*
*Sponge*
*Gold pigment*
*Acrylic varnish*
*Small paintbrush*
*Clear gloss varnish*

**1** Prepare the cupboard. Apply two coats of white matt emulsion paint. Scale up and cut out the fleur-de-lys motif template.

Place the template on the top of the cupboard and draw around it using a pencil. Repeat this process on the door.

**2** Mix a base colour that is a mid-tone with a mixture of green acrylic and white matt emulsion paint. Cover the whole piece of furniture using a large paintbrush. Paint carefully around the fleur-de-lys motif so that it remains white. Leave this to dry for 1 hour.

**3** Mix a darker shade of green, using more green acrylic and less white matt emulsion paint. Place a small quantity of paint on a dish so that it can be spread out thinly. To keep the fleur-de-lys motif white, cover it with the original template. Sponge the darker green up to the edge and onto the paper. Work quickly and lightly all over the cupboard to ensure that there is an even pattern and texture.

**4** While the green is drying, mix the gold pigment and acrylic varnish to form a liquid gold. Then paint the fleur-de-lys using a small paintbrush. It may need two coats to ensure it is covered completely.

**5** When the gold is dry, paint a shadow and further detail on the fleur-de-lys in a dark green acrylic colour with a small paintbrush. Allow 30 minutes for the paint to dry completely.

**6** Then apply a coat of clear gloss varnish using a large paintbrush.

# PAINTING CHINA
# TECHNIQUES

### Ceramic enamels

Painting decorative designs on china can be very rewarding, but you must take care to use non-toxic ceramic enamels and always keep your painted designs away from areas that will come into contact with foodstuffs, such as the rims and insides of mugs and cups.

The range of ceramic enamel paints for china decoration is constantly being refined and developed, so be sure to follow the manufacturer's instructions carefully about the use and application of the particular brand you have selected.

The instructions will also give details of how to fix your design to make it more permanent and how to clean brushes and other equipment.

### Preparing surfaces

Make sure the china surfaces you wish to decorate are clean and dry. First wash the china in hot, soapy water, then rinse well with clean water and allow to dry naturally. Newly purchased china should be wiped down with a solution of 600 ml (1 pt) warm water and 10 ml (2 tsp) vinegar. This will remove any greasy fingerprints from the surface.

The same solution can also be used for cleaning wall tiles prior to painting.

### Types of paint

There are various types of paint you can use for decorating china. Cold ceramic enamels need no fixing, but they are not always suitable for surfaces which may come in contact with food and require a coat of varnish to help protect the design from the knocks of everyday life. Other ceramic enamels are gently heated and fixed when the design is dry using a domestic oven.

### Brushes

Use artists' paintbrushes for applying the design. Although sable brushes are considered to be the best, they are very expensive. Instead, you could choose brushes filled with either squirrel hair or synthetic bristles. Whichever type of brushes you buy, clean them carefully and thoroughly after use before the ceramic enamels have a chance to dry hard in the bristles. Certain types of ceramic enamels are water-soluble, so brushes and containers can be simply washed out in warm, soapy water but others may need a solvent, usually white spirit or paint thinner, to remove the paint. Check the manufacturer's instructions for the particular paint you are using. Store cleaned brushes upright on their handles in a clean container.

### Applying the decoration

To avoid smudges, allow each area of your design to dry before moving onto the next (*right*). Take care to wipe off any mistakes immediately while the ceramic paint is still wet. When choosing a brush to paint a particular area, match the size of the brush to the shape you are covering – if in doubt, always go for a slightly smaller brush size than you think you will need. Do not overload your brush with colour as this can create drips and runs of paint, and keep your brush moving in one direction (*left*).

### Aftercare

Remember that the designs on china that you paint at home will be much less permanent than those on the decorated kiln-fired china you buy in the shops. This is especially true when designs are painted with water-soluble colours. Wash painted pieces gently in luke-warm, soapy water and do not rub with a cloth or a scourer. Allow to drain and dry naturally.

To make the decorations on vases and bowls more permanent, seal them with two coats of clear polyurethane varnish. The varnish will help protect the design from scratches and chips when the objects are in use. Never use this sealing technique on items designed for food.

# CUP AND SAUCER

The appeal of the bold design on this cup and saucer is its look of spontaneity. If you do not feel confident enough to copy the fluent brush strokes, practise on a piece of broken china. Unless you are absolutely certain that the paints you are using are food-safe, adapt the design by stopping the decoration at least 4 cm (1½ in) below the rim of the cup.

### YOU WILL NEED
*Non-toxic ceramic enamels*
*Small paintbrush*
*White spirit*
*White china cup and saucer*

**1** Dip the brush in green ceramic enamel and make bold squiggles on the cup. Leave to dry. Clean the brush before changing colours using white spirit. Between the green shapes paint purple squiggles. Leave to dry.

**2** Decorate other white spaces with red ceramic paint. Paint red dots on the handle. Decorate the saucer in the same way.

*Painting China*

# FEEDING TIME

It is not easy to find attractive bowls for pets, so why not decorate a brightly coloured one with cold enamels? You might like to write your pet's name on the bowl too, to personalize it. Make absolutely certain that you use non-toxic enamels, and only paint the outside of the bowl, *not* the inside.

## YOU WILL NEED
China bowl
*600 ml (1 pt) warm water with 10 ml (2 tsp) vinegar*
*Chinagraph pencil*
*Cold ceramic enamel*
*Small paintbrush*

**1** Wash the bowl in the vinegar solution to remove any grease. Dry thoroughly. Draw your design directly onto the bowl with a chinagraph pencil.

**2** Paint around the design with enamel colour.

**3** Paint a row of fine spots around the outside edge of the bowl.

# THAT'S TORN IT

This is a very easy way of giving an inexpensive china mug a distinctive design. You can also decorate a plate to match. Make absolutely sure the ceramic enamels are non-toxic.

## YOU WILL NEED
*Tape measure*
*China mug*
*Masking tape*
*Scissors*
*Non-toxic ceramic enamels*
*Small paintbrush*

**1** Measure the circumference of the mug and cut three strips of masking tape. Rip the masking tape in half lengthways and place it with the straight edges back to back round the mug in bands.

**2** Press the masking tape down so that the paint can not seep under the edges. Apply ceramic enamel to the white areas. Leave to dry overnight.

**3** Peel off the masking tape.

### WARNING
Take care with the selection of paints. Not all ceramic paints and enamel paints are non-toxic or food-safe. Always study the manufacturer's instructions carefully and follow them exactly. If you have the slightest doubt, NEVER paint any surface that will come into contact with food or the lips or mouth. To adapt a design such as this you would stop the decoration at least 4 cm (1½ in) below the rim of the cup.

# TERRACOTTA PLANTER

Brighten up a plant collection with a set of unusually decorated terracotta flowerpots. The clay absorbs some of the colour to create an attractive matt effect. Try experimenting with patterns and colours to create a whole range of designs.

## YOU WILL NEED
*Terracotta flowerpot*
*Pencil*
*Tape measure*
*Small paintbrush*
*Assorted ceramic enamels*

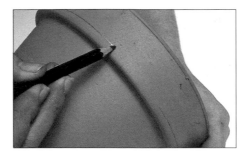

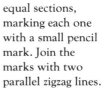

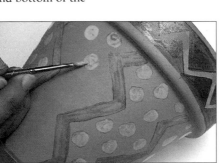

**1** Using a pencil, draw two parallel horizontal lines around the top and bottom of the rim of the flowerpot. Keep the lines as straight as possible.

**3** Using a small paintbrush, paint the zigzags in one colour and the surrounding area of the rim in a contrasting shade. Mark in vertical zigzags in pencil on the side of the flowerpot and paint in. Paint dots inbetween. Leave to dry.

**2** Calculate the circumference of the rim with a tape measure and divide it into an uneven number of equal sections, marking each one with a small pencil mark. Join the marks with two parallel zigzag lines.

# FANCY TILES

Why not brighten up your bathroom with the minimum of fuss by decorating the tiles? If you use cold enamels that set without heating, you can paint tiles that are already in place — just remember to follow the manufacturer's instructions, and let the tiles dry thoroughly before you take a bath or shower!

## YOU WILL NEED
*Ceramic tiles*
*600 ml (1 pt) warm water with 10 ml (2 tsp) vinegar*
*Chinagraph pencil*
*Cold ceramic enamels in a variety of colours*
*Paintbrushes in various sizes*
*Tile adhesive and grout (optional)*

**1** Wash the tiles down with the vinegar solution to remove any grease. Dry thoroughly. Draw your design directly onto the tiles in chinagraph pencil. Any mistakes can be easily removed with a piece of paper or your fingers.

**2** Start to fill in the largest area of your design with enamel, using a fairly thick brush. Work quite loosely, as you can add fine details when the first coat of enamel is dry.

**3** Add definition to your design by painting on top of the first colour with a darker-toned enamel.

**4** If you want a bold effect, outline your design with black enamel. If you are painting loose tiles, stick them in position with tile adhesive. When the adhesive is thoroughly dry add the grouting. Do not allow the tiles to come into contact with water for at least 48 hours.

# CANAL BOAT MUG

This colourful mug would make a perfect gift for any canal boat enthusiast. The stylized form of decoration is a traditional feature not only of the boats, but also of buckets and other utensils.

## YOU WILL NEED
*Small paintbrush*
*Ceramic enamels*
*Enamel mug*
*White spirit*

**1** Dip the brush in ceramic paint and paint circular shapes onto the mug as a background for the roses. Leave to dry. Clean the brush before changing colours using white spirit. Paint circles in other colours to form a design.

**2** Paint petals on the roses and turn some of the shapes into leaves. Emphasize the detail with black or white ceramic enamels.

**3** Outline the design with red dots and paint a wavy red line on the handle.

# CHRISTMAS CANDLE HOLDERS

Why not create decorative candle holders especially for the festive season? Green holly leaves and red berries are quite easy to paint directly onto the china, using a sprig of fresh holly as a pattern.

## YOU WILL NEED
*Plain white candle holder*
*Red and green ceramic enamels*
*Small paint brush*
*White spirit (paint thinner)*

**1** Paint outlines of the holly leaves in green ceramic enamel all round the candle holder, then fill in each leaf in the same colour. Leave to dry.

**2** Clean the brush before changing colours using white spirit. Paint red berries between the leaves.

# PLANT POT IN RELIEF

Many pieces of china are available with patterns that are raised or 'in relief'. The detail can be further emphasized by colouring the design in ceramic paint, perhaps in the shades suggested by the patterns on the china or even to match a particular interior decor scheme. Cold ceramic enamels are easy to apply but it is best to avoid painting china used for food.

## YOU WILL NEED
*China pot with relief design*
*Cold ceramic enamels in different*
  *colours*
*Small paintbrush*
*Clear polyurethane varnish*

**1** Wash the china pot in warm soapy water to remove any grease or grime. Allow to dry thoroughly.

Choose a colour scheme and apply the first shade of paint carefully using a small paintbrush.

**2** Paint in the areas chosen for the second colour, wiping off any paint that might go over the edge of a particular detail.

**3** Continue to paint in the design until the china pot is decorated all over.

Allow the paint to dry thoroughly. For extra protection apply a coat of clear varnish.

# DESIGN IN THE NEGATIVE

Draw on a white plate with a black chinagraph pencil and then colour the remaining areas. The chinagraph pencil marks are then rubbed away, leaving white lines in their place. Make sure the ceramic enamels are of the non-toxic variety.

## YOU WILL NEED
*Black chinagraph pencil*
*White china plate*
*Ceramic enamels*
*Small paintbrush*
*Paper towel or tissue paper*

**1** Using the chinagraph pencil, draw your design onto the plate.

**2** Paint in the larger areas of colour. If you wish to mix colours, make sure you mix enough. Ceramic enamels look better slightly dappled, as it is very difficult to achieve a flat even surface over a large area.

**3** When the large areas have been painted, fill in the details. Do not overload the brush with paint but build up the colour gradually. Leave the paint to dry. Rub away the chinagraph pencil marks using a paper towel or tissue paper.

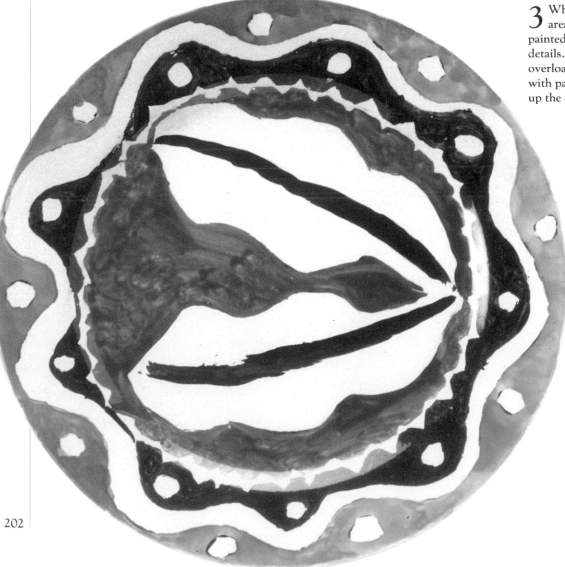

# EGGCUPS

These eggcups will help to get your day off to a good start! They are bright and jazzy, and take their inspiration from European folk art designs. As when painting all crockery, make absolutely sure that you are using non-toxic cold ceramic enamels, and do *not* paint any surface that comes directly into contact with food. Bon appetit!

## YOU WILL NEED
600 ml (1 pt) warm water with 10 ml
    (2 tsp) vinegar
Chinagraph pencil
Plain white eggcups
Cold ceramic enamels in a variety of
    colours
Paintbrushes in various sizes

**1** Wash each eggcup in the vinegar solution to remove any grease. Dry thoroughly. Draw your design directly onto the china using a chinagraph pencil.

**2** Start to fill in the first colour of enamel. Work from the lightest shades to the darkest, so that you can paint on top of initial coats of enamel if you like.

**3** Continue to paint in the design.

**4** For a bolder effect, first block in the design with bright colours, and then outline with black enamel.

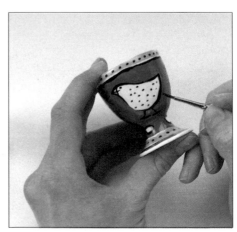

# STENCILLING TECHNIQUES

## Stencil materials

The choice of stencil material depends on the project you are undertaking – a masking tape or plain paper stencil is fine used once, but for stencilling repeating patterns it is best to use a durable material. Clear acetate is the best choice as it is hard-wearing, completely transparent and easy to clean – choose .0075 gauge as this is thin enough to cut easily and it can withstand a great deal of handling. Oiled stencil paper and stencil card are available from arts and crafts shops – these are easier to cut than acetate, but tend to be more difficult to position accurately because they are opaque.

## Cutting your stencil

There are several ways of cutting a stencil: you can draw your design freehand onto the stencil material with a black felt-tip pen, trace it from the source directly onto clear acetate, or use cut-out paper shapes as templates to cut round. Use a craft knife (available from arts and crafts shops) with a new blade when cutting your stencil (*below*), and always take care to place your work on a special cutting surface to avoid damaging furniture. A large piece of glass, scrap wood or heavy card makes a good cutting surface, or you may decide to buy a special cutting mat with a self-healing surface. A

good cutting mat will last for several years, even with heavy use, and its special surface makes the work of cutting accurate stencils much easier.

When cutting, try to cut in a continuous line, turning the stencil slowly so you are always cutting towards you and lifting the knife blade from the stencil as little as possible. Remember that the knife blade should be directly on the design line, not inside or outside it. When your design has been cut out completely, hold the stencil up to the light and check it thoroughly. Make sure that you have cut out all the shapes required and also correct any jagged edges.

## Applying paint

The consistency of paint for stencilling is important, whether it is applied with a stencil brush or a sponge. Thick, dry paint is difficult to apply evenly while wet, runny paint will seep under the stencil material and cause the edges of the shape to distort and blur. Apply the colour lightly with very little paint on the brush using a dabbing and brushing movement. Experiment on a piece of scrap paper until you achieve the desired result.

You can stencil shapes with a single colour of paint to make a crisp, neat design or you may prefer to build up a design using several colours applied one after the other to the same cut-out shape: this gives a gradual change of tone across the design (*left*).

## Brushes and paints

Stencil brushes made from natural bristles are available from arts and crafts stores. They have short, rather stiff bristles and are available in a wide range of sizes. Pieces of sponge can also be used (*below*), and this will give a soft, blurry effect.

Paints for stencilling are either oil- or water-based and the two types should not be mixed together. They can be thinned if necessary – water-based paints with cold water and oil-based types with white spirit – but take care to do this gradually, one or two drops at a time.

## Finishing off

Always let one area of stencilling dry before moving your stencil to another position. Depending on the type of paint you are using, drying time can take anything from a few minutes to several hours.

After stencilling, clean brushes and containers immediately using warm, soapy water for water-soluble paints and the appropriate solvent for oil-based types. Remove as much paint as possible from acetate or card stencils, let them dry thoroughly and store them flat for future use.

# PLANT POT

A fern or other non-flowering house plant looks very effective in this plain white pot with a bold stencilled design.

## YOU WILL NEED
*15 cm (6 in) white china plant pot*
*4 cm (1½ in) wide masking tape*
*Pencil*
*Craft knife*
*Ceramic enamels in 2 basic colours*
*Small plate for paints*
*2 small pieces of sponge*
*Plastic glove*

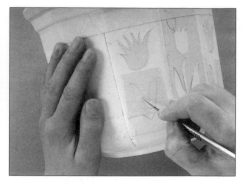

**1** Cover the rim of the pot with masking tape, overlapping the outer edge by 12 mm (½ in). Cover the side of the pot with masking tape, leaving a 4 cm (1½ in) space between each strip of tape. Draw a flower design on each strip of tape and pencil in the parts to be cut out.

**2** Holding the pot firmly with one hand, take the craft knife with the other and carefully cut out the shapes drawn onto the masking tape. Peel off the cut-out tape as you go along. Continue until the design is complete all round the pot.

**3** Pour a little paint onto a plate. Using a small piece of sponge, dab the first colour onto alternating cut-out spaces. Repeat with the second colour. Wear a plastic glove on the hand you use to apply the paint to protect yourself from splashes. Sponge under the rim and around the base of the pot. Leave to dry thoroughly. When dry, peel off all the masking tape.

# STENCILLED TRINKET BOX

This charming trinket box can be used to keep many things such as coins, keys or spare buttons. The traditional method of stencilling enables you to repeat a design quickly and easily.

## YOU WILL NEED
*Round box*
*White matt emulsion paint*
*Small paintbrush*
*Pencil*
*Plain paper*
*Tape measure*
*Clear acetate*
*Black felt-tip pen*
*Craft knife*
*Masking tape*
*Blue acrylic paint*
*Stipple brush*
*Clear polyurethane varnish*

**2** Lift the stencil carefully and tape it down onto the lid. Stipple it with undiluted blue acrylic paint, using a dry stipple brush. Leave to dry.

**3** Repeat this process for the side design, remembering to tape down the stencil, moving it around the box as necessary.

**1** Prime the box with a coat of white matt emulsion paint. Draw around the lid onto a sheet of plain paper to get the correct size for the design. Measure the circumference and depth of the box and transfer these measurements onto the paper. Scale up the design within the measurements. Place the box lid on the acetate, draw around it with a felt-tip pen and then cut out the shape. Stick down the acetate onto the lid design with masking tape. Cut out the stencil with a craft knife. Repeat this process to make the stencil for the side design.

**4** Paint the rim of the lid with blue acrylic paint. Leave to dry and then coat with clear polyurethane varnish to protect the box.

# STENCILLED NOTELETS

Choose a pattern that will look good repeated on the head of the notelets. If you have not used stencils previously, it is best to practise on newspaper before working on expensive writing paper.

## YOU WILL NEED
*Sheets of coloured writing paper*
*Strip of stiff card*
*Pencil*
*Scissors*
*Assorted poster paints*
*Small plate*
*Small round stencil brush or small*
*     sponge*
*Soft cloth*

**1** Fold the sheets of writing paper in half. Take the strip of card and concertina into 15 mm (⅝ in) folds.

**2** Keep the card folded and draw out a pattern. Cut out using scissors. Open the pattern out flat and lay it across the top of the folded writing paper.

**3** Mix a little poster paint on a small plate. Dab the stencil brush or sponge into the paint, wiping off any surplus on a soft cloth. It is very important not to overload the brush or sponge with paint if you want to avoid smudges. Place the cut-out card onto the head of the folded sheet of writing paper, holding the card firmly in position with one hand. Dab paint through the opening of the cut-outs. Lift up the card gently and leave the paper to dry.

# ROSE CARD

This romantic birthday card is very effective, particularly on the black background colour which adds depth to the stencilled single rose.

## YOU WILL NEED

*Square of stiff card*
*Ruler*
*Pencil*
*Plain paper*
*Masking tape*
*Clear acetate twice the size of the folded card*
*Craft knife*
*Natural sponge*
*Assorted acrylic paints*
*Small paintbrush*

**1** Fold the square of stiff card in half, scoring along the inside line. Measure the front of the card to ensure your design fits the available space. Draw a rose design onto plain paper, taping it down onto a clean flat board. Cover the design with half of the acetate and tape down. Cut out only the shape of the rose. Remove the stencil carefully. Move the acetate up so that the bottom half covers the design. Repeat the cutting process, only this time cut out only the shape of the leaves.

**2** Place the stencil of the leaves onto the card, securing with the masking tape and making sure the stencil is central. Moisten the natural sponge, squeezing out any excess water. Use green and white acrylic paint for the leaves, making sure the paint is not too wet. Fade the sponging from the edge towards the middle of the leaves. Leave to dry and remove carefully.

**3** Place the stencil of the rose carefully onto the centre of the card, moving it around until it fits snugly in the middle of the bed of leaves. Repeat the process with pink and white acrylic paint, again fading the stippling with the natural sponge in towards the middle. Leave to dry and remove the acetate carefully.

**4** Add a finishing touch with a twirl of paint using a paintbrush, and your card is completed.

# COSMIC STATIONERY

The intricate design of shooting stars and fireworks demands neat fingers and plenty of patience! Use the stencil to make a harlequin set of writing paper in a variety of colours.

## YOU WILL NEED
*Strip of stiff card*
*Masking tape*
*Pencil*
*Craft knife*
*Sheets of coloured writing paper*
*Poster paint in assorted colours*
*Round stencil brush or small sponge*
*Soft cloth*

**1** Cover a strip of stiff card completely with strips of masking tape. Using a pencil draw a design of shooting stars and fireworks on it. Working on a hard-surfaced board and using a craft knife cut out all the shapes carefully to form the stencil template.

**2** Place the stencil over a sheet of writing paper, and secure in position with a little masking tape. Have your paints ready on a plate. Dab the brush or sponge into each colour, wiping off any surplus on a soft cloth. It is very important not to overload the brush or sponge with paint if you want to avoid smudges. Dab the paints through the stencil until the design is completed. Lift up the stencil gently and leave the paper to dry.

# STENCILLED TRAY

The traditional technique of stencilling is an extremely effective form of decoration. This tray is pretty enough to be displayed in your kitchen when not in use. Why not try using colours to match a favourite set of china?

## YOU WILL NEED
*Wooden tray*
*White matt emulsion paint*
*Large paintbrush*
*Sandpaper*
*Masking tape*
*Diluted blue acrylic paint*
*Stipple brush*
*Sheet of plain paper*
*Pencil*
*Clear acetate*
*Craft knife*
*Clear satin polyurethane varnish*

**1** Prepare the tray. Prime with white matt emulsion paint, rub down with sandpaper and give it another coat for a nice smooth finish. When the paint is dry, put masking tape all along the inside edges of the tray. Brush diluted blue acrylic paint thinly onto the edges of the tray and stipple off while the paint is still wet; work swiftly and only do a section at a time so that the paint does not have a chance to dry.

**2** Draw your design onto plain paper, stick the paper down onto a smooth board and then place a sheet of acetate on top, making sure you stick it down on top of the design with masking tape. Place on a hard surface and start to cut out the shapes of your stencil very carefully, using a craft knife and holding down the acetate with your free hand where necessary.

**3** When you have finished cutting out the design, transfer the stencil onto the tray, remembering to remove the masking tape very carefully. Tape down the stencil in the centre of the tray. It is also a good idea to tape down some paper around the edges of the acetate so that splashes of blue do not go on to the surrounding area. Stipple on the paint with a dry stipple brush using fairly dry acrylic paint; get rid of any excess paint before beginning by stippling on a scrap of paper. Leave to dry, remove the stencil and give the tray two coats of clear satin polyurethane varnish.

# PHOTO FRAME

Jazz up a favourite photograph with a simple stencilled frame. Choose colours that enhance those in the photograph and mount it on the wall for all to see. If a stencil is made for one frame, it can be used again to make a series.

## YOU WILL NEED
*Thick coloured card*
*Metal rule*
*Craft knife*
*Thin card*
*Clear acetate*
*Permanent black ink pen*
*Masking tape*
*Stencil brush*
*Acrylic paint*
*Clear glue*
*Picture hanger*

**1** First draw up the pieces of your frame on thick coloured card. Then carefully cut these out using a metal rule and craft knife. In the same way, cut three spacers out of thin card.

**2** Take a piece of clear acetate of the same width as the front frame piece and draw on the design with a permanent black ink pen. Then cut out the design with a sharp craft knife.

**3** Place the acetate on the front frame piece, securing it with masking tape. Using a stencil brush with a little acrylic paint, stipple on the paint. Allow the paint to dry before removing the acetate.

**4** Glue the three spacers onto the sides and the bottom to the back of the stencilled frame piece. Then stick the spacers to the back piece of coloured card frame.

**5** When the frame is complete, attach a light picture hanger to the back, strengthen with masking tape, and hang on the wall.

# STAR SCARF

Stencilling a plain scarf is a wonderful way to show off your artistic talent and look original.

## YOU WILL NEED
*Thin card*
*Clear acetate*
*Permanent black ink pen*
*Craft knife*
*Scarf*
*Masking tape*
*Fabric paints*
*Stencil brush*
*Iron*
*Tissue paper*

**1** Make a star template in thin card to fit the scarf. Draw round the template onto clear acetate using a permanent black ink pen. Cut out the star image from the clear acetate, following the black lines using a craft knife.

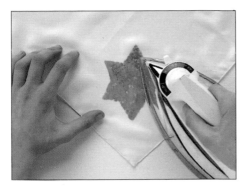

**2** Secure the acetate stencil on a corner of the scarf with masking tape. Put a little fabric paint onto the stencil brush and stipple the paint straight onto the fabric. Start at the tip of each star point and lightly work towards the middle. Concentrate more on the points and edges to get a 3-dimensional look.

**3** Repeat on all four corners and the centre of the scarf and allow to dry. Iron the star images with a medium hot iron. Place a piece of tissue paper between the iron and the fabric to protect the paint. The heat of the iron fixes the fabric paint so that it can be washed.

# SEAHORSE SHIRT

Transform a white cotton turtle-neck with a stencilled design of an exotic seahorse painted in three bright colours.

## YOU WILL NEED
*Thin card*
*Craft knife*
*Black felt-tip pen*
*Thick card cut to turtle-neck size*
*White cotton turtle-neck*
*Masking tape*
*3 round stencil brushes*
*Fabric paints in 3 colours*
*Small plate*
*Fine flat brush*

**1** Cut a piece of thin card to fit the area of the front of the turtle-neck you would like to decorate. Scale up the design to the required size. Insert the thick card inside the shirt to stretch the fabric, and prevent the paint from leaking onto the back.

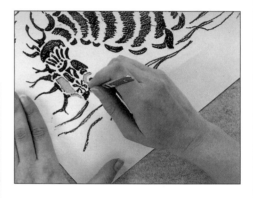

**2** Place the design on a hard-surfaced board and cut out all the black shapes carefully. This is your stencil.

**3** Secure the stencil on the front of the turtle-neck using masking tape. Hold the stencil brush vertically and dab the paint through the cut-out holes of the stencil. Change colours and brushes as you go along. When you have finished colouring the design lift up the stencil carefully and put it aside to dry. If there are any smudges, touch up carefully with a fine flat brush. Leave the turtle-neck to dry thoroughly. Remove the piece of thick card. Fix according to the instructions on the paints.

# FLOWER POT STENCIL

Enhance your plant with an individual flower pot. Decorate a terracotta plant pot to give it individuality; try varying the sizes for a whole collection.

## YOU WILL NEED
*Terracotta flower pot*
*Clear acetate*
*Permanent black ink pen*
*Craft knife*
*Masking tape*
*Acrylic paint*
*Small stencil brush*

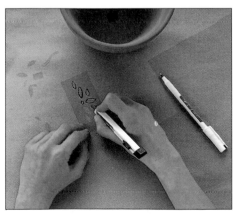

**1** Wash the flower pot thoroughly with soapy water so that all grease and dirt marks are removed. Leave to dry thoroughly. Scale up the flower design from the template. Then draw it onto clear acetate with a permanent black ink pen. Cut around the black pen lines on the acetate carefully using a sharp craft knife.

**2** Secure the acetate stencil onto the terracotta flower pot with masking tape. Then apply the acrylic paint directly onto the terracotta pot through the acetate, using a stencil brush. Use small amounts of paint; if too much is applied, it may leak under the acetate. Do not remove the acetate until the paint is dry.

**3** Move the acetate stencil around the pot repeating the process until you are satisfied with the total design. Clear acetate has the advantage of your being able to see through it for perfect placement when spacing your design.

# SCENTED
## AND
# EDIBLE GIFTS

# FLOWERCRAFT TECHNIQUES

## Materials

Fresh flowers can play an important part in adding a personal touch to home decorations, but the arrangements quickly fade and die, particularly in centrally heated rooms. Equal pleasure can be gained from the use of preserved and artificial flowers and foliage to decorate a room, particularly flowers such as roses and lavender which retain their perfume when dried. The flowers, leaves and seed-heads of most garden plants can be preserved at home, often just by hanging bunches up to dry naturally in the air, and a home-dried crop (*left*) can be supplemented and enhanced by the addition of commercially dried plants together with realistic silk flowers, leaves and artificial fruits.

Flowers and leaves are easy to press at home, and the results can be arranged into stunning designs for pictures and greetings cards or be used to decorate wax candles and other objects.

## Equipment

Florist's foam, wire, putty, tape and pin holders (*right*) are reasonably inexpensive and easy to obtain from a florist's shop or garden centre. All these items are immensely useful in helping you to achieve the desired results when working with dried flowers. You may also decide to buy some of the more specialized equipment such as a pair of florist's wire cutters, although it is quite possible to improvise with household tools which are to hand.

### Drying flowers at home

The simplest method of drying flowers is by air drying. Simply group your chosen flowers into loose bunches and hang them up to dry in a cool, dry room (temperature not less than 10°C [50°F]) with good air circulation. The best places are an attic or loft, a garage, a frost-free shed, or a spare room, providing it is not centrally heated. When hanging the bunches up to dry, make sure that air can circulate freely round the flowers, leaves and stems in order to avoid rotting.

### How to press flowers

Pressing flowers (*below*) is one of the easiest ways of preserving flowers at home and pressed petals are simple to arrange and glue, using rubber-based adhesive. You can buy a traditional type of flower press from a craft shop, or make your own from two squares of heavy-duty plywood joined at the corners with four long bolts and securing wing nuts. Make sure the bolts are long enough to accommodate several sheets of cardboard and blotting paper when the press is filled.

Gather your flowers on a dry day and place them in the press as soon as you can. Avoid plants which have fleshy stems and leaves and large, three-dimensional flowers which would become distorted by pressing. Place the flowers and leaves to be pressed between two sheets of thick white blotting paper (available from good stationery shops), then stack the sheets in the press, separating each 'sandwich' with a spacer sheet of thick cardboard.

Large sprays of foliage can be pressed beneath the carpet – lay the foliage between sheets of newspaper and place under the carpet. This method works especially well with ferns, although you should take care not to choose an area of floor which forms part of a busy thoroughfare – too much treading will result in broken leaves. Small flowerheads and single leaves can also be pressed between the pages of a heavy book, but remember to sandwich the plants first between sheets of blotting paper.

Whichever method of pressing you use, check on the results after about 10 days. Some plant materials will take longer to dry out than others and if you are unsure that the drying process is complete, simply replace the layers and wait for a few more days.

# CAT CUSHION

Most 'bean bag' cushions are very popular with pets, but this one with its additional filling of catmint (irresistible to cats) with tansy and cotton lavender (which fleas and other fur 'visitors' hate) should make for a very happy cat.

## YOU WILL NEED

*Lengths of cotton and calico (muslin) fabrics*
*Scissors*
*Needle and thread*
*½ cupful of dried tansy*
*½ cupful of dried catmint (nepeta)*
*½ cupful of dried cotton lavender (santolina)*
*1 heaped teaspoon of orrisroot powder*
*Small polystyrene (styrofoam) 'pearls' for filling*

**1** Cut out two pieces each of the calico (muslin) and your chosen cotton outer cover fabric, measuring 50 cm × 41 cm (19½ in × 16 in). Stitch the two short sides and one long side of the calico together, and part of the remaining long side, leaving a 7.5 cm (3 in) opening. Turn through. Repeat with the cover fabric, remembering to start with the material inside out. Leave a bigger opening so that the filled calico inner can be inserted.

**2** Mix the tansy, catmint, cotton lavender and orrisroot powder together in a bowl. Make up a calico sachet about 10 cm (4 in) square, fill with the special cat pot-pourri and sew together. Fill the calico inner with the polystyrene 'pearls', pop in the sachet and sew together.

**3** Slide the calico-covered cushion into the outer cover and slipstitch the gap.

# POT·POURRI

This simple and lightly spiced pot-pourri has a careful selection of material, chosen for its appearance in a basket as well as for its perfume.

## YOU WILL NEED

3 cupfuls dried blue larkspur flowers, a few dried red roses for colour, 1 cupful geranium leaves, 1 cupful of soapwort leaves and flowers

1 teaspoon grated lemon rind

½ teaspoon sandalwood powder for smell

½ cupful orrisroot powder (perfume fixative)

Mixing bowl

5 drops of geranium essential oil for smell

Plastic ice-cream container with tight-fitting lid

Sticky tape

Display bowl or basket

Lace ribbon

**1** Remove the larkspur florets from the stems and break up the roses, reserving some whole for decoration.

**2** Add the geranium leaves, soapwort leaves and flowers, lemon rind, sandalwood and orrisroot powders.

Place all the ingredients in a mixing bowl and stir gently as you slowly drip in the geranium essential oil.

**3** Transfer the mixture to a plastic ice-cream container and seal the lid carefully with sticky tape. Store in a warm place for 6 weeks, stirring occasionally. When the pot-pourri is ready, empty into a display bowl, or fill a small basket. Decorate with a small bunch of larkspur and roses tied with a lace ribbon.

# TABLE DECORATION

This soft, delicate arrangement is an ideal table decoration for a small or intimate dinner party and a chance to display that very special plate.

## YOU WILL NEED
Florist's adhesive clay tape
Florist's scissors
Plastic pin holders
Small pretty plate
Florist's plasticine (putty)
2 plastic candle holders
Scrim ribbon
Silver and black reel wires
Florist's wire cutters
Reindeer moss
Dried larkspur
Fir cones
Dried roses
Candles

**1** Cut a short length of florist's adhesive clay tape and use it to fix a florist's plastic pin holder off-centre on your chosen pretty plate.

**3** Cut several 15 cm (6 in) lengths of scrim ribbon and form into single loops using silver reel wire.

**2** Knead a piece of florist's plasticine (putty) into a 5 cm (2 in) diameter ball and fix onto the pin holder. Push two plastic candle holders into this.

**4** Cut 5 cm (2 in) pieces of silver reel wire and bend into hairpin shapes. Cover the candle holders and clay with pieces of reindeer moss, securing it in place with the wire pins.

**5** Wire the larkspur and fir cones using black reel wire.

**6** Cut down rose stems to suitable lengths. Start to place the various elements, by pushing into the florist's plasticine (putty). Insert the ribbon loops to simulate bows and disguise the candle holders. Finally place the two candles in their holders. Take great care not to let lighted candles burn down near the decorations.

# SCENTED NOTEPAPER

The tradition of 'scenting' notepaper goes back many centuries; often a drop of the sender's favourite scent was used but this stained the paper. It is much better to leave a lavender sachet with the paper for a month.

## YOU WILL NEED
*Muslin (cheesecloth)*
*Needle and thread*
*½ cupful lavender flowers*
*Handmade or fine acid-free notepaper*
*Pressed flowers*
*Tweezers*
*Rubber-based adhesive*
*Toothpick*
*Box or bag*
*Sticky tape*
*Cellophane*

**1** Make up a square sachet of muslin and fill with lavender.

**2** Decorate the notepaper using pressed flowers. Arrange the flowers or petals using tweezers, sticking them in place with a dab of rubber-based adhesive applied with a toothpick.

**3** Put the notepaper in a box – or a bag if you do not have a box big enough – with the sachet and seal the box. Leave for a month. Take the notepaper out of the box or bag, and wrap it in cellophane to keep in the perfume.

# PRESSED FLOWER CANDLE

Making these candles is challenging, but good fun. Turn a plain white candle into an elegant decorated gift that will give hours of pleasure.

## YOU WILL NEED
*Heatproof cylindrical container (taller and wider than the candle)*
*4-5 cm (1½-2 in) diameter white candle*
*Selection of pressed flowers, leaves or grasses*

**1** Fill the container with enough hot water to reach the shoulder of the candle when it is immersed. Holding the candle by the wick, immerse in the hot water for about 30 seconds. Remove the candle, and working quickly, press a few leaves and flowers onto the softened wax around the lower part of the candle.

**2** Refill the container with very hot water and dip the candle again briefly to soften the wax surface and seal in the pressed flowers.

# ROSEBUD POMANDER

This long-lasting pomander looks beautiful and its perfume can be renewed when necessary with a few drops of rose essential oil.

## YOU WILL NEED

90 cm × 12 mm (36 in × ½ in) green satin ribbon
Length of florist's wire
9 cm (3½ in) diameter florist's foam (styrofoam) ball
Dried rosebuds of different sizes
White woodworking glue or rubber-based glue
Paste brush
Rose essential oil

**1** Cut the ribbon into 3 equal lengths. Tie a bow in the centre of each piece of ribbon leaving two long ends. Tie the third piece into a double bow and leave the ends long to make a hanging loop. Twist a florist's wire around each bow leaving one long end and push the wires through the foam ball. Pull the bows down to the ball and tuck in the end of each wire to secure.

**2** Grade the rosebuds from smallest to largest. Divide the ball into quarters by painting a line of glue and pressing in a row of medium-sized rosebuds along it.

**3** Cover one quarter at a time with glue and press in rosebuds, the smallest at the top and bottom and getting larger as you reach the centre, until the ball is completely covered. A few drops of rose essential oil can now be dripped onto the pomander ball.

Winter months are the time to use the flowers that you pressed in the summer. It is fun arranging them into a picture, which makes such a lasting gift when covered with protective film, available from specialist suppliers. Folded cards are available from most artist's suppliers.

## YOU WILL NEED
*Rubber-based adhesive*
*Small dish*
*Selection of dried flowers including verbena, forget-me-not, spiraea and gypsophila (baby's breath) and foliage*
*Folded blank card with aperture*
*Tweezers*
*Toothpick*
*Heat-sealing protective covering film*
*Steam iron*

**1** Squeeze out a little adhesive onto a small dish. Start by positioning foliage in an irregular oval shape to fit within the cut-out aperture of the card. Fix the foliage in position using tweezers to pick up each leaf. Using a toothpick transfer the smallest spot of adhesive to the reverse side of the leaf and touch it down.

**2** Position and touch down verbena and forget-me-not flowers in the same way.

**3** Use florets of spiraea and gypsophilia (baby's breath) to complete your design.

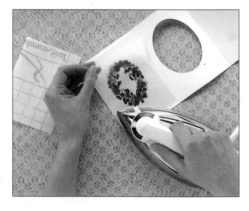

**4** Protect the design with iron-on heat sealing laminate. Cut out a piece of the laminate slightly smaller than the page size. Open up the card and cover the design with the sheet of protective film, and iron down in accordance with the manufacturer's instructions. Re-fold the completed card.

# FESTIVE WREATH

The materials and colours for this wreath have been chosen to suit any festival or occasion from an anniversary or birthday to Christmas. All the items are readily available from craft or florist's suppliers. A spring or summer wreath can be made using the flowers available.

## YOU WILL NEED
*Florist's scissors*
*Dried nigella orientalis seed-heads*
*Florist's foam (styrofoam) wreath base*
*Florist's wire cutters*
*Bunches of artificial fruit and leaves*
*Dried ambrociana*
*Florist's black and silver reel wires*
*Lace ribbons*
*Dried red roses*

**1** Cut short stems of nigella orientalis, and insert around the inner circumference of a foam wreath at an angle of about 15°.

**2** Cut down the wires of the bunches of artificial fruit and leaves to about 4 cm (1½ in) in length, and insert around the top of the wreath at regular intervals.

**3** Wire together small bunches of ambrociana with florist's black reel

wire and insert all around the outside of the wreath to form a soft edge.

**4** Cut eight 30 cm (12 in) lengths of ribbon to make bows with two loops and two ends. Bind with florist's silver reel wire, leaving two ends, and insert evenly

around the wreath. Then cut five 12.5 cm (5 in) lengths. Fold in half, bind with florist's silver reel wire at the centre and insert around the outer edge of the wreath.

**5** Position the roses evenly around the centre of the wreath and fill in with more

nigella and ambrociana where required to give a balanced effect.

# LAVENDER BAG

These lavender bags, smelling so fresh and clean, make very pretty gifts that look charming and are so practical in a linen cupboard.

## YOU WILL NEED

35 cm × 6 mm (14 in × ¼ in) ribbon
28 cm × 5 cm (11 in × 2 in) piece of lace
Scissors
4 pieces of muslin (cheesecloth), each 12.5 cm × 10 cm (5 in × 4 in)
Needle and thread
Lavender pot-pourri
5 stems of lavender
Small elastic band

**1** Cut a 12.5 cm (5 in) length of ribbon and lace. Place a length of lace and one of ribbon 7.5 cm (3 in) from the bottom edge of a piece of muslin (cheese-cloth) and stitch into place. Gather the remaining length of lace and stitch to the top of the muslin.

**2** Turn through and stitch the sides. Fold to the centre seam, stitch the bottom edge and turn through.

**3** Fill with the lavender pot-pourri and tuck the five stems of lavender into the top of the bag, protruding from the neck, and secure with an elastic band.

**4** Take the remaining ribbon and tie in a bow around the neck, to cover the elastic band.

# FLOWER POSY

The posy is a very old form of flower arrangement with its origins dating from the medieval nosegay. Using dried and silk flowers means it can be treasured as a keepsake for years to come.

## YOU WILL NEED

*Florist's foam (styrofoam) posy holder and ready-formed lace frill*
*Dried gypsophila (baby's breath)*
*Florist's scissors*
*Florist's silver reel wire*
*Florist's wire cutters*
*Stems of silk peony flowers, buds and leaves*
*Sticky tape*
*2.5 cm (1 in) wide length of cream silk ribbon*

**1** Fix the frill around the foam head of the holder by pulling it down until it is firmly in place.

**2** Cut short heads of gypsophila and wire together with silver reel wire.

**3** Remove the leaves from the peony stems and insert a row around the edge of the foam block.

**4** Cut the stem of a peony bud and insert into the centre of the foam block, and position open flowers around the edge.

**5** Add more leaves and peonies. Fill in by inserting bunches of wired gypsophila to create an even but soft effect.

**6** Tape the ribbon to the end of the handle and bind upwards towards the under-side of the posy. Secure with sticky tape. Make several 'figures of eight' from the remaining ribbon and bind at the centre to form a multiple bow. Wire to the base of the posy to cover the back. Stick down.

# HERBAL BATH SACHETS

These scented sachets hang under the hot water when the bath tub is being filled. They create a refreshing fragrance as well as being naturally soothing and softening for the skin.

## YOU WILL NEED

1 cupful oatmeal
½ cupful powdered milk
¼ cupful wheat bran
Handful of dried lavender or
    rosemary flowers
Handful of soapwort leaves and
    flowers
Plastic bowl
Teaspoon
Nappy (diaper) liners or thin
    cheesecloth
6mm (¼ in) wide ribbon or string
Pinking shears

**1** Mix all the ingredients together in a plastic bowl.

**2** Place two teaspoons of the mixture in the centre of a nappy (diaper) liner. Gather up the liner around the mixture and tie with a ribbon or string, leaving ends long enough for the sachet to hang beneath the running water.

**3** Cut off the corners of the nappy liners using pinking shears and arrange so that you achieve a pretty frill.

# SCENTED
# SHELLS

As sea shells are generally associated with water, the ideal place to display a collection is in the bathroom. Add a further pleasing dimension to their colour and form by making them fragrant.

## YOU WILL NEED
*Collection of sea shells*
*Dish-washing liquid*
*Bleach*
*Towel*
*1 vanilla pod (bean)*
*Small cuttlefish bone*
*Lemon, bay and rosemary essential*
 *oils*
*Plastic ice-cream container with tight-*
 *fitting lid*
*Glass dish or bowl*

**1** Scrub and wash the shells carefully in soapy water to which a little bleach has been added, and set aside to dry thoroughly on a towel.

**2** Moisten a cuttlefish bone with 25 drops of lemon, 15 drops of bay and 5 drops of rosemary essential oils. Place a bruised vanilla pod and the cuttlefish bone into a plastic ice-cream container. Add the shells, seal down the lid and leave for 4 weeks. Remove half the shells and arrange in a glass dish or bowl for display. After a few weeks or whenever the shells lose their fragrance, replace with the other shells left in the container. Do this on a regular basis, and occasionally refresh the cuttlefish bone with a few drops of the essential oils.

# ALMOND BUBBLE BATH

This bubble bath makes a delightful gift – it is excellent for the skin, adds a beautiful perfume and foams when a little is poured slowly under fast-running hot water, when you are starting to fill the bathtub. It also looks good displayed in the bathroom.

### YOU WILL NEED
*300 ml (½ pint) non-biological*
*    dishwashing liquid*
*Screw-top jar*
*15 drops peach essential oil*
*2 drops pink food colouring*
*2 tablespoons almond oil*
*Presentation bottle*
*Label*

**1** Pour the dishwashing liquid into the screw-top jar and add the peach essential oil and food colouring.

**2** Add the almond oil, screw on the lid and shake vigorously for about a minute. Fill the presentation bottle immediately. Decorate the bottle as liked and label carefully with a list of the contents and instructions to shake the bottle for a few seconds before use.

*SUGGESTED LABEL:*

## ALMOND BUBBLE BATH

A mild soap base combines with peach essential oil to produce foaming frothy pink bubbles for a gentle soak in the bath tub.

# SWEET VIOLET CREAM

This sweet-smelling rich beauty cream makes an interesting change to the usual commercially produced cosmetics.

## YOU WILL NEED

1 teaspoon beeswax
3 tablespoons almond oil
Heatproof mixing bowl
Small saucepan
Newspaper
½ teaspoon cornflour (cornstarch)
2 tablespoons boiling water
Balloon or electric whisk
6 drops violet essential oil
Presentation jar
Label

**1** Melt the beeswax in the almond oil in a bowl over a saucepan of hot water. When melted, remove the bowl and stand on some folded newspaper.

**2** Add the cornflour (cornstarch), stir well and then add the water gradually, beating with the whisk until the mixture becomes creamy.

**3** Add the violet essential oil, and continue to whisk until the cream is cool. Then pour into the presentation jar and leave to set. Label with a list of the contents.

# SPICE AND LEMON COLOGNE

This cologne with its fresh, spicy aroma makes a super gift for any man. The miniature bottles are ideal for packing when travelling.

## YOU WILL NEED
*2 handfuls of lemon geranium leaves*
*Sharp knife*
*2 cinnamon sticks*
*Screw-top jar for mixing*
*3 teaspoons grated lemon rind*
*1½ cups vodka (or ethyl alcohol)*
*Coffee filter paper*
*Plastic or glass funnel*
*Small glass jug*
*Presentation miniature bottles*
*Labels*

**1** Wash the geranium leaves, pat dry and chop finely. Break up the cinnamon sticks and pack with the leaves into the jar. Add the grated lemon rind to the jar and fill with vodka. Secure the lid and store in a warm place for 4 weeks, shaking daily.

**2** Filter the mixture through a coffee filter paper in a funnel into a jug. Repeat if the liquid is not very clear.

Wash and dry the storage jar and pour in the filtered cologne. Put the lid on the jar and keep in a dark place for 6 months.

**3** Taking care not to disturb any sediment, decant the liquid carefully into the miniature bottles and label with the contents.

# ROSE MOISTURIZER

This moisturizer, made from natural ingredients, is light, nourishing and soothing and will make a most welcome gift.

## YOU WILL NEED
1 teaspoon beeswax
3 teaspoons lanolin
Small heatproof mixing bowl
Small non-aluminium saucepan
3 tablespoons almond oil
150 ml (¼ pint) rose-water
Pinch of borax
Cooking thermometer
Balloon whisk
Screw-top presentation jar
Label

**1** Melt the beeswax and lanolin in a small mixing bowl resting in the saucepan of hot water over a low heat. Add the almond oil and beat together. Put the mixing bowl in a warm place.

**2** Wash and dry the saucepan. Heat the rose-water and borax to about 50°C (122°F) and add slowly to the mixing bowl. Whisk the mixture together.

**3** Stand the bowl in cold water and continue whisking until the cream is cold. The cream will still be soft and can be spooned into the presentation jar. Label with a list of contents.

# AROMATIC BODY OIL

Almond oil can be bought inexpensively in large quantities from specialist shops. It is very light and soothing to the skin and is specially beneficial with this exotic blend of essential oils. Remember that essential oils are very strong, and should never be used undiluted directly on the skin. If some is splashed on by accident, wash it off immediately with soap and water. The body oil can be used after baths, or rubbed on elbows, knees and hands at any time.

## YOU WILL NEED
*150 ml (¼ pint) almond oil*
*Screw-top jar for mixing*
*15 drops peach essential oil*
*10 drops melissa essential oil*
*Presentation bottles*
*Labels*

**1** Pour the almond oil into the screw-top jar.

**2** Add the peach and melissa essential oils, drop by drop. Secure the lid and shake for 1 minute. Leave for 1 hour before pouring into the presentation bottles. Label with contents.

*SUGGESTED LABEL:*

### AROMATIC BODY OIL

A refreshing and soothing body oil for use after bathing or on dry skin at any time, with the delicate scents of peach and melissa essential oils.

# PEPPERMINT FOOT-BATH

This rejuvenating pick-me-up for tired and aching feet would be much appreciated by a busy hostess hard at work. The given quantity will be enough for four foot-baths. To use, fill a large bowl with moderately hot water, stir in the peppermint mixture and soak the feet for 10 minutes.

## YOU WILL NEED
*Several stems of fresh peppermint or 60 g (2 oz) dried peppermint leaves*
*125 g (4 oz) juniper berries*
*Non-aluminium saucepan with lid*
*750 ml (1¼ pints) water*
*12 drops sandalwood essential oil*
*6 drops cypress essential oil*
*Coffee filter paper*
*Funnel*
*Storage jars or bottles*
*Labels*

**1** Place the peppermint and juniper in the saucepan, add the water and heat slowly to just below boiling point, stirring occasionally. Cover the saucepan and leave to cool.

**2** Before the mixture is cold, add the sandalwood and cypress essential oils and stir well.

**3** Strain off the liquid through a coffee filter paper in a funnel into the storage jars. Seal and label with instructions on how to use and a list of contents.

# ROSEMARY HAIR RINSE

This rosemary rinse should be massaged into the scalp as a final rinse to make the hair beautifully soft and well-conditioned.

## YOU WILL NEED
*2 handfuls of fresh rosemary stems*
*2 jars with plastic screw-tops*
*600 ml (1 pint) white vinegar*
*600 ml (1 pint) water*
*Non-aluminium saucepan*
*Coffee filter paper*
*Funnel*
*Presentation bottles*
*Labels*

**1** Wash the rosemary stems carefully in cold water and shake dry. Break into manageable lengths and divide between the jars.

**2** Put the vinegar and water in a saucepan and bring to the boil. Leave to stand for 2 minutes and pour over the rosemary in the jars. Stand on a warm window-sill for 2 weeks, shaking occasionally. Then strain the liquid through a coffee filter paper in a funnel into the presentation bottles. Label with a list of the contents and instructions on how to use.

# SCENTED BATH SALTS

This is a very easy way to make beautifully scented, coloured bath salts. You can use any colouring and any variety of essential oil you like.

## YOU WILL NEED
3 tablespoons vodka
Small yogurt pot
Pink food colouring
Peach essential oil
1 teaspoon almond oil
Plastic spoon
1 kg (2 lb) washing soda crystals
1 litre (1¾ pint) plastic ice-cream
    container with a well-fitting lid
Presentation jars
Ribbon
Labels

**1** Pour the vodka into the clean yogurt pot, and add about 5 drops of pink food colouring, 15 drops of peach essential oil and the almond oil. Stir until the mixture is thoroughly blended.

**2** Put the washing soda crystals into the ice-cream container, give the vodka mixture a final stir, and pour it over carefully. Keep turning the crystals over with a plastic spoon for a few minutes, and then seal with the lid.

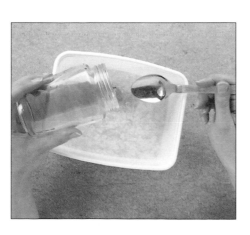

**3** After 3 days, stir the bath salts again and pack into attractive jars. Add a ribbon bow and label with the contents.

# MARINATED OLIVES

A jar of these marinated olives makes an original hostess gift. As they will cause a minor explosion on the palate, warn people when offering them at a drinks party with other nibbles!

## YOU WILL NEED
*Jar of pitted black olives in brine*
*Jar of pitted green olives in brine*
*Sieve*
*1 fresh hot chilli*
*3 cloves of garlic*
*Chopping board and knife*
*Storage jar*
*5 ml (1 tsp) dried oregano*
*Olive oil*
*Presentation jar*
*Label*

**1** Empty the jars of olives into a sieve and rinse thoroughly under a running cold tap. Set aside to drain. Chop the chilli and garlic very finely and put into the storage jar with the oregano. Add a little oil and shake well.

**2** Add the drained olives and enough oil to cover. Shake gently for a minute every day for a week, then transfer to the presentation jar, topping up with more olive oil if necessary. Label the jar, listing all the ingredients.

# ALMOND TREATS

While these 'fruits' are traditionally eaten at Christmas, they also make a super gift at any time of the year. Try to use white marzipan (almond paste) which will enable you to mix more realistic colours.

## YOU WILL NEED
*White marzipan (almond paste)*
*Sharp knife*
*Board*
*Rolling pin*
*Gel food colourings*
*Icing (confectioners') sugar*
*Toothpicks*
*Petits fours paper cases*
*Lidded container*
*Greaseproof (wax) paper*

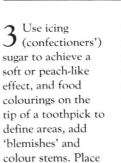

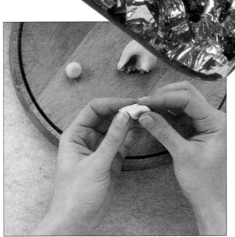

**1** Divide the marzipan (almond paste) into pieces for the basic colouring. Roll out ⁓ne piece thinly. Dot the food colouring very lightly on the surface. Then knead the marzipan (almond paste) until it is evenly coloured. Repeat this process for each colour.

**2** Mould the marzipan (almond paste) into appropriate fruit shapes to suit the different colours. Use a little extra colouring in some areas.

**3** Use icing (confectioners') sugar to achieve a soft or peach-like effect, and food colourings on the tip of a toothpick to define areas, add 'blemishes' and colour stems. Place the fruit in petits fours cases to protect them and enhance their appearance. Store in a lidded container, lined with grease-proof paper, until they are packed into a presentation box.

# HERB BUTTER

Decorative containers filled with herb-flavoured butters make thoughtful gifts for busy cooks. Rosemary butter is good with green peas and roast lamb, mint with new potatoes, and fennel with fish.

## YOU WILL NEED
*Fresh herbs of your choice*
*Paper towels*
*Chopping board*
*Sharp knife or herb chopper*
*Best quality unsalted butter*
*Salt*
*Saucers or small mixing bowls*
*Spatula*

**1** Rinse small bunches of herbs carefully in cold water and pat dry with paper towels. Chop each herb very finely on a chopping board, keeping each herb separate.

**2** Cut up the unsalted butter into medium-sized pieces and allow to soften at room temperature. Sprinkle a little salt over the herbs — this will help to crush the herbs and release their flavour.

**3** Mix the herbs with the softened butter using a spatula. When thoroughly mixed together pack into decorative containers and chill in the refrigerator until required.

# GINGERBREAD TREES

*Try baking a light gingerbread mixture in decorative Christmas tree shapes, and edge with icing (confectioners') sugar 'snow'. Finish them off with pretty seasonal ribbon bows.*

### YOU WILL NEED
*100 g (4 oz/1 stick) butter, slightly softened*
*100 g (4 oz/⅔ cup) soft brown sugar*
*100 g (4 oz/½ cup) golden (corn) syrup*
*2 eggs*
*Sieve*
*450 g (1 lb/4 cups) white self-raising flour*
*15 ml (1 tbsp) ground ginger*
*Rolling pin and board*
*Christmas-tree shape cutter*
*Baking sheet*
*Ribbon*
*Shallow dish*
*Icing (confectioners') sugar*

**1** Beat the butter, sugar and golden (corn) syrup into a cream and then beat in the eggs. Sift in the flour and ground ginger and mix into a dough.

**2** Roll the dough out thinly and stamp out Christmas tree shapes. Arrange on an oiled baking sheet. Bake for 20 minutes at 180°C (350°F/gas 4).

**3** When cool, tie a ribbon bow on each tree shape and then dip the sides carefully in a shallow dish containing about 6 mm (¼ in) depth of icing (confectioners') sugar to decorate the upper edges of the branches with 'snow'.

# ROSE AND JASMINE TEAS

Both rose and jasmine teas are lightly but beautifully flavoured, are drunk without milk, and are delicious either hot or cold. Dried rose and jasmine petals are available from specialist suppliers. Green 'gunpowder' teas are made with large leaves which, like the petals, will sink, so they are suitable for using when making tea directly in a cup or glass. Only use half a teaspoon for each cup.

## YOU WILL NEED
*Rose petals*
*Net bag*
*Lemon zest-peeler or sharp knife*
*Lemon*
*Plate*
*Dried jasmine petals*
*Gunpowder tea*
*Airtight storage containers*

**1** To dry your own rose petals, choose a variety that is sweet rather than bitter-tasting. Half-fill a little net bag with rose petals and hang in a warm dark place until dry.

**2** Using a lemon zest-peeler or a sharp knife, remove only the zest (no pith) from a lemon, shred finely and leave to dry on a plate in the bottom of a cooling oven for 30 minutes.

**3** Combine equal parts by weight first of dried rose petals and gunpowder tea, and then of jasmine petals and the tea, adding a quarter part of dried lemon zest to the jasmine mixture. Store the teas in separate airtight containers.

# HERB-INFUSED OILS

Now lighter, healthier dressings for salads are popular, these delicately flavoured oils make very welcome gifts. It is best to use only one variety of herb in each bottle of oil, but oregano and basil do go well together. Olive or sunflower oil is recommended, or use walnut or grapeseed for a gourmet treat.

## YOU WILL NEED
*Stems of fresh rosemary, thyme, oregano or basil*
*Paper towel*
*Attractive presentation bottles*
*Plastic or glass funnel*
*Scissors*
*Fine quality salad oils of your choice*
*Self-adhesive labels*

**1** Choose only the freshest stems of herbs, wash in cold water and pat dry on a paper towel.

**2** Using a funnel, fill the bottles with the chosen oils. Using scissors, trim the herbs to about two-thirds the height of the chosen bottles, and discard any discoloured leaves, but leave any flowers – dead or alive. Insert the herbs into the bottles.

**3** Seal the bottles and label with the ingredients. Leave for two months before use.

# CHOCOLATE FUDGE

This is a beautiful rich fudge, made in the traditional way. It will make a delectable gift for anyone with a sweet tooth.

## YOU WILL NEED

*450 g (1 lb/2¼ cups) granulated sugar (preferably cane)*
*150 ml (¼ pint/⅔ cup) milk*
*50 g (2 oz/¼ cup) cocoa powder*
*50 g (2 oz/2 squares) dark chocolate*
*Saucepan*
*6 drops vanilla essence (extract)*
*150 ml (¼ pint/⅔ cup) double (heavy) cream*
*100 g (4 oz/½ cup) unsalted butter*
*Shallow non-stick baking sheet*
*Metal spatula*
*Sharp knife*
*Gift boxes*

**2** The mixture will now be thick. Transfer to an oiled non-stick shallow baking sheet and spread out evenly using a metal spatula. Leave to set for 12 hours in a cool place.

**1** Heat the sugar, milk, cocoa and chocolate in a pan, stirring until the mixture has dissolved. Add the vanilla essence, cream and the butter, then re-heat stirring occasionally until the butter melts. Remove from the heat and beat with a wooden spoon until the fudge mixture starts to granulate.

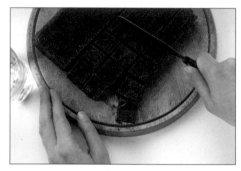

**3** Invert the fudge onto a chopping board and cut into even squares, frequently dipping the knife blade in water. Pack into your chosen gift boxes.

# TANGY VINEGARS

Flavoured red wine or cider vinegars are invaluable in preparing many dishes, sauces and dressings. They keep well for several months after maturing, but should be stored away from bright light. Here are recipes for tarragon vinegar and red chilli with ginger vinegar. Alternatives are numerous: try making a salad dressing with grapeseed oil and ginger and garlic vinegar, or tarragon vinegar and yogurt with cold chicken; or black pepper, coriander and cardamom vinegar in a meat stew; and red chilli and cumin vinegar on fried fish.

## YOU WILL NEED
*Fresh tarragon stems*
*Screw-topped bottle of cider vinegar*
*Whole dried red chillies*
*Fresh ginger root*
*Screw-topped bottle of red wine*
  *vinegar*
*Ribbon for decorating*
*Self-adhesive labels*
*Felt-tip pen*

**1** Trim three freshly picked tarragon stems to fit under the surface of the cider vinegar, and put into the bottle.

**2** Place two whole red chillies and two small pieces of ginger root in a bottle of red wine vinegar.

**3** Screw the lids onto the bottles, decorate with ribbon and add labels listing the ingredients. Store in a dark cool place for at least a month.

# BOUQUET GARNI

The traditional bouquet garni is
made from three sprigs of parsley,
two of thyme and a bay leaf tied
together with string, and often
enclosed in muslin (cheesecloth) so
that it can easily be removed. Other
herbs may be added, such as fennel
for fish dishes, three sage leaves
for pork dishes, four short sprigs of
rosemary for lamb dishes, two sprigs
of fresh coriander (cilantro) and an
extra bay leaf for beef dishes.

### YOU WILL NEED

*Sprigs of fresh or dried parsley and
    thyme*
*Bay leaf*
*Sharp pointed scissors*
*Muslin (cheesecloth)*
*White string*

**1** Mix together
three parts
chopped parsley, two parts chopped
thyme and one part
broken bay leaves.

**2** Cut out circles
of muslin
(cheesecloth) 9 cm
(3½ in) in diameter. Put two heaped teaspoons of the herbs
into the centre of
each circle.

**3** Gather the
muslin around
the herbs and tie in
little bundles with
white string. Store
in an airtight
container.

# CHERRIES IN BRANDY

Only use the best quality canned cherries as cheaper varieties might split open in the brandy. A decorative jar filled with perfect fruit makes a most acceptable hostess gift.

## YOU WILL NEED

*1 can best quality pitted red cherries*
*    in syrup*
*Can opener*
*Small saucepan*
*1 cinnamon stick*
*3 tablespoons granulated cane sugar*
*Wooden spoon*
*Strainer*
*2 screw-top jars (sterilized)*
*¼ bottle of cooking brandy*
*3 drops vanilla essence (extract)*
*Small jug*
*Fancy lidded glass jar (sterilized)*
*Ribbon*
*Label*

**1** Drain the syrup from the cherries into a saucepan, add the cinnamon stick and sugar and stir continuously while bringing to the boil. Allow to cool and strain off into one of the screw-top jars and store in the refrigerator.

**2** Reject any damaged fruit and place the remainder in the other screw-top jar.

Add the brandy and vanilla essence. Screw on the lid and store in a cool place for 3-4 weeks.

**3** Pour off the brandy into a jug, and stir in small quantities of the chilled syrup to taste. Place the cinnamon stick in the fancy glass jar and pack in the fruit in a decorative manner. Fill the container with the sweetened brandy, seal and finish with a ribbon bow. Add a label listing the ingredients.

# STOCKISTS AND SUPPLIERS

FABRICS, SEWING, QUILTING
AND HABERDASHERY SUPPLIES

Borovicks
16 Berwick Street
London
W1V 4HP
UK
(071) 437 2180
(Glitzy fabrics and silk)

Chartwell Graph Paper
H W Peel & Co Ltd
Chartwell House
1C Lyon Way
Rockware Estate
Greenford
Middlesex
UB6 0BN
UK
(081) 578 6861
(Isometric graph paper)

Chattels
53 Chalk Farm Road
London
NW1 8AN
UK
(071) 267 0877
(Quilts and fabrics)

Crimple Craft
1 Freemans Way
Forest Lane
Wetherby Road
Harrogate
HG3 1RW
UK

DMC Creative World
Pullman Road
Wigston
Leicester
LE18 2DY
UK
(Threads and cottons)

Framecraft Miniatures Ltd
148-150 High Street
Aston
Birmingham
B6 4US
UK
(021) 359 4442
(Craft boxes)

Green Hill
27 Bell Street
Romsey
Hants
SO51 8GY
UK

Harlequin
Lawford
Manningtree
Essex
CO11 1UX
UK
(Covered buttons)

Leicester Laminating Services
71 Westfield Road
Weston Park
Leicester
LE3 6HU
UK
(Plastic graph and template material)

Magpie Patchworks
Department G
37 Palfrey Road
Northbourne
Bournemouth
Dorset
BH10 6DN
UK

Maple Textiles
189-190 Maple Road
Penge
London
SE20 8HT
UK
(081) 778 8049

Patchworks and Quilts
9 West Place
Wimbledon
London
SW19 4UH
UK
(Quilts and fabrics)

Piecemakers
13 Manor Green Road
Epsom
Surrey
KT19 8RA
UK

Pioneer Patches
Marsh Mills
Luck Lane
Huddersfield
Yorkshire
HD3 4AB
UK

Pongees Ltd
184-186 Old Street
London
EC1V 9BP
UK
(071) 253 0428
(Silk merchants)

Quilt Basics
2 Meades Lane
Chesham
Bucks
HP5 1ND
UK

The Quilt Room
20 West Street
Dorking
Surrey
RH4 1BL
UK

Silken Strands
33 Linksway
Gatley
Cheadle
Cheshire
SK8 4LA
UK
(Embroidery requisites)

The Stitchery
6 Finkle Street
Richmond
North Yorkshire
DL10 4QA
UK

Strawberry Fayre
Chagford
Devon
TQ13 8EN
UK
(Mail order fabrics)

Threadbear Supplies
11 Northway
Deanshanger
Milton Keynes
MK19 6NF
UK
(Waddings/battings)

George Weil & Sons Ltd
18 Hanson Street
London
W1P 7DB
UK
(071) 580 3763
(Silk paints and equipment)

George Weil & Sons Ltd
The Warehouse
Reading Arch Road
Redhill
Surrey
RH1 1HG
UK
(0737) 778868
(Silk paints and equipment. Shop, mail
order and export)

DMC Corporation
Port Kearny
Building 10
South Kearny
New Jersey 07032
USA
(*Threads and cottons*)

P & B Fabrics
898 Mahler Road
Burlingame
California 94010
USA

DMC Needlecraft Ltd
PO Box 317
Earlswood
NSW 2206
Australia
(*Threads and cottons*)

Auckland Folk Art Centre
591 Remuera Road
Remuera
Auckland
New Zealand
(09) 524 0936

Fibre Flair
Main Road
Waikanae
New Zealand
(04) 293 6035

Quilt Connection Ltd
214 Knights Road
Lower Hutt
New Zealand
(04) 569 3427

The Craft Lady
47 Bramley Gardens
Corlett Drive
Bramley
Johannesburg
South Africa
(11) 440 2519

Faysons Art Needlework Centre
135a Greenway
Box 84036
Greenside
Johannesburg
South Africa
(11) 646 0642

KNITTING AND CROCHET
YARN SUPPLIES

Arnotts
Argyle Street
Glasgow
UK
(041) 248 2951

John Lewis
Oxford Street
London
W1A 1EX
UK
(071) 629 7711

Liberty
Regent Street
London
W1R 6AH
UK
(071) 734 1234

Rowan Yarns
Green Lane Mill
Holmfirth
West Yorkshire
UK
(0484) 681881

Christa's Ball & Skein
971 Lexington Avenue No.1A
New York
New York 10021
USA
(212) 772 6960

Greenwich Yarns
2073 Greenwich Street
San Francisco 94123
USA
(415) 567 2535

Hook 'N' Needle
1869 Post Road East
Westport
Connecticut 06880
USA
(203) 259 5119

Mariposa
826 E California Boulevard
Pasadena
California 91106
USA
(818) 405 8805

Mixed Media
2531 Rocky Ridge Road No.101
Birmingham
Alabama 35243
USA
(205) 822 5855

Straw Into Gold
3006 San Pablo Avenue
Berkeley
California 94702
USA

Westminster Trading Corporation
5 Northern Boulevard
Amherst
New Hampshire 03031
USA
(*Yarn by mail order*)

Woolworks
6305 Falls Road
Baltimore
Maryland 21209
USA
(410) 337 9030

A Knit Above
2427 Granville Street
Vancouver
V6H 3G5
Canada
(604) 734 0975

Imagiknit
2586 Yonge Street
Toronto
M4P 2J3
Canada
(416) 482 5287

Indigo Inc
155 Rue St Paul
Quebec City
G1K 3W2
Canada
(418) 694 1419

Greta's Handcrafts Centre
25 Lindfield Avenue
Lindfield
NSW 2070
Australia
(02) 416 2488

Mateira
250 Park Street
Victoria 3205
Australia
(03) 690 7651

Pots 'N' Stitches
113 London Circuit
ACT 2600
Australia
(062) 487 563

John Q. Goldingham Ltd
PO Box 45083
Epuni Railway
Lower Hutt
New Zealand
(04) 567 4085

Randburg Needlework
19 Centre Point
Hill Street
Randburg
South Africa
(11) 787 3307

## ARTS SUPPLIES AND SPECIALIST PAPERS

Dylon International Ltd
Worsley Bridge Road
London
SE26 5BE
UK
(081) 650 4801
(*Fabric dyes and pens*)

Falkiner Fine Papers Ltd
76 Southampton Row
London
WC1B 4AR
UK
(071) 831 1151

Robert Horne Paper Company
Huntsman House
Mansion Close
Moulton Park
Northampton
NN3 1LA
UK

T N Lawrence & Son
119 Clerkenwell Road
London
EC1R 5DA
UK
(071) 242 3534

One Four Nine Paper Supplies
PO Box A13
Huddersfield
West Yorkshire
HD3 4LW
UK
(*Mail order specialist*)

Paperchase
213 Tottenham Court Road
London
W1A 4US
UK
(071) 580 8496

Paperpoint
130 Long Acre
London
WC2E 9AL
UK
(071) 379 6850

Paperpoint
26 Calthorpe Road
Edgbaston
Birmingham
B15 1RP
UK

Kate's Paperie
8 West 13th Street
New York
New York 10001
USA

Papersource Inc
730 N Franklin Suite 111
Chicago
Illinois 60610
USA

ACT Papers Pty Ltd
10 McGlone Street
Micham
Victoria 3132
Australia

E & F Good
31 Lansdowne Terrace
Walkerville
SA 5081
Australia
(08) 344 4306

Karori Art, Craft and Wallpaper
  Centre
264 Karon Road
Karori
New Zealand
(04) 476 8426

Littlejohns
170 Victoria Street
Wellington
New Zealand
(04) 385 2099

G Webster & Co Ltd
44 Manners Street
Wellington
New Zealand
(04) 385 4136

Academy of Crafts
28 Goldman Street
Florida
South Africa
(11) 472 4884

Art Book Centre
45C Bok Street
PO Box 23982
Joubert Park 2044
South Africa
(11) 725 1498

Arts and Crafts Depot
40 Harrison Street
Johannesburg
South Africa
(11) 838 2286

## DECOUPAGE SUPPLIES

The Dover Bookshop
18 Earlham Street
London
WC2H 9LN
UK
(071) 836 2111

Hawkin & Co
Saint Margaret
Harleston
Norfolk
IP20 0PJ
UK
(0986) 82536
(*Decoupage scraps by mail order*)

Panduro Hobby Ltd
West Way House
Transport Avenue
Brentford
Middlesex
TW8 9HE
UK
(081) 847 6161
(*Hatboxes by mail order*)

Dover Publications Inc
31 East 2nd Street
Mineola
New York 11501
USA
(212) 255 3755

Paper E Clips
20 Maud Street
Suite 307
Toronto
Ontario M5Y 2M5
Canada
(416) 941 9075

Rosenhain, Lipmann & Peers Pty
147 Burnley Street
Richmond
Melbourne
Victoria 3121
Australia
(03) 428 1485

The Partners
St Martins Stationery
5 Austin-Kirk Lane
Christchurch 2
New Zealand

## CERAMIC PAINTS AND SUPPLIES

Art Graphique
Unit 2 Poulton Close
Dover
Kent
CT17 0HL
UK
(304) 242244

Potterycraft Ltd
Harrison Bell
Campbell Road
Stoke-on-Trent
ST4 4ET
UK
(0782) 272 444
(*White china blanks*)

Reeves Art Shop
178 Kensington High Street
London
W8 7RG
UK
(071) 937 5370

A.R.T. Studio Clay Company
1555 Louis Avenue
Elk Grove Village
Illinois 60007
USA
(708) 593 6060

Ceramic Supply of New York and
New Jersey Inc
534 La Guardia Place
New York
New York 10012
USA
(212) 475 7236

Duncan Ceramics
5673 East Shields
Fresno
California 93727
USA
(209) 291 2515

## PRESSED AND DRIED FLOWER SUPPLIES

Swancraft Gallery
Ashfield
Stowmarket
IP14 6LU
UK
(0728) 685703
(*Pressed and dried flowers and pot-pourri supplies by mail order*)

Flowers Forever
Queensgate
Knights Road
Lower Hutt
New Zealand
(04) 566 5830

## HERBS AND ESSENTIAL OIL SUPPLIES

G Baldwin & Co
173 Walworth Road
London
SE17 1RW
UK
(081) 703 5550

Butterbur & Sage Ltd
Greenfield House
21 Avenue Road
Southall
Middlesex
UB1 3BI
UK
(081) 574 3737

Crafte Supplies
33 Oldridge Road
London
SW12 8PN
UK
(081) 673 6370

Field & Co (Aromatics) Ltd
Stonefield Close
South Ruislip
Middlesex
HA4 0LA

Sussex Herbs
34-36 Cliffe High Street
Lewes
BN7 2AN
UK
(0273) 471125

# INDEX

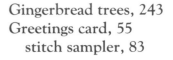

# CONTRIBUTORS

*Mary Lawrence* is a specialist in flowercrafts and edible and scented gifts, and runs a flourishing pressed flower and craft gallery in the county of Suffolk. A florist by training, she supplies craft enthusiasts and flower arranging experts through a worldwide mail order and advice network.

*Marion Elliot* is one of Great Britain's leading papier-mâché artists, and specializes in original paper sculptures and accessories in distinctive colours. She has her work exhibited at Liberty's of London, and has contributed to many books on the art of modelling with paper.

*Emma Whitfield* specializes in the art of decoupage, particularly the decorating of hat boxes. Trained in Fine Art, she undertakes commissions for Harrods, London's most famous department store and exhibits at prestigious craft fairs around Great Britain.

*Josephine Whitfield* is a specialist in decorated furniture and restoration. Her distinctive work is shown at the leading craft fairs. She employs her training in Fine Art to transform everyday objects into pieces of distinctive beauty.

*Annette Claxton* is one of Great Britain's best-known quilters. She has travelled to the United States and Australia to demonstrate her art. Her sewing expertise combined with a flair for originality and colour allows her to turn her hand to dressmaking, appliqué and patchwork as well.

*Freddie Robins* teaches textiles in colleges of art and design in Great Britain, and specializes in millinery

and innovations in knitwear. Her scarves are often commissioned by leading department stores in London, and her work is to be seen frequently in the top fashion magazines such as *Elle Decoration*.

*Jan Eaton* is the author of several stunning books on the art of needlepoint, cross stitch and embroidery. As well as teaching crafts and textile arts, Jan continually creates new designs and writes extensively.

*Ariane Gastambide* is a stage and costume designer, travels widely with theatre companies in Europe, Japan, South America and Australia, gathering ideas for her unusual and beautiful creations. Specializing in masks and puppetry, Ariane is also a gifted painter and needlewoman.

*Juliet Moxley* is a professional fashion and textile designer and studied at Camberwell School of Art in London. She has written many books on art, style and design, and enjoys making the projects she researches, constantly putting new ideas into practice.

*Rina da' Prato* is a well-known knitwear designer and crochet expert and her fashion creations are often featured in magazines such as *Vogue* and *Cosmopolitan*. Rina's designs are commissioned by leading department stores and are also featured in the famous Rowan Yarns collections.

*Jan Bridge* is a talented seamstress; she fashions *objets d'art* from fabric and natural materials. A contributor to many craft magazines and several books on handicrafts Jan undertakes a variety of sewing commissions for various publications.